"*Unleashing Intellectual Capital* is a daring ⸺ opens our minds and demonstrates how our inherent genetic tendencies can be leveraged for competitive advantage. This book provides the reader with new and useful ammunition in which to operate in the new millennium."

—**John W. Patten**, President Emeritus, *Business Week*

"Dr. Ehin is the rarest of business authors: the subject expert whose writing is clear, focused, and actionable. *Unleashing Intellectual Capital* is a must read for tomorrow's business winners."

—**David Stauffer**, President of Stauffer Bury Inc.

"[A]n absolutely fascinating work which must be read by all contemporary managers. This book not only points the way for future global business evolution, but truly is a 'capstone work' which draws from Dr. Ehin's professional expertise, and also incorporates all of his life's experiences into an exceptional 'common-sense approach' to the science of management for the new millennium. . . . Personally, I believe that the elements that he sets forth provide an exceptional sound basis to guide all managers well into the future."

—**Peter F. Gerity**, Vice President for Research,
Utah State University

"Charlie Ehin has done us all a great favor. He has clearly demonstrated that in the long run there can be no middle ground between controlled and shared access based organizations. And he has shared with us the precious knowledge that organizations flowing from a shared access foundation are those more likely to succeed in very unpredictable environments. Those who do not see a clear connection between the 'new science' and how human endeavors ought to be 'scientifically' organized should read this book."

—**Ned Hamson**, Senior Editor, *The Journal for
Quality and Participation*

"In *Unleashing Intellectual Capital* Dr. Ehin has developed a model that will help create the necessary competitive advantage for companies through intellectual capital generation. He has provided the keys that open the best in an individual, team and a company as a whole. His book is the key to success for all change managers and anyone else interested in prospering in the Knowledge Age."

—**Carl Champagne**, President and CEO,
Data Systems International, Inc.

"Dr. Ehin's *Unleashing Intellectual Capital* is a rare treasure in the evolution of management theory. Never before have we enjoyed a more comprehensive, integrated framework for managing human assets that incorporates the critical components necessary for success in the new millennium."

—Carol C. Leavitt, Sunstone Partners

"In this day and age of rapid change in both society and scientific endeavor, we all begin to see a convergence of biology, sociology, world economy, computer science, etc. I admire your courage in trying to amalgamate these diverse facets of human-kind and lead the reader to the obvious 'right and good' choice for our society and our enterprise structure."

—Donald F. Summers, M.D., Associate Director,
National Cancer Institute

"Finally a book which not only brings back today's complex world of work to a human dimension, but reveals explicitly that in our basic humanness lies a source of incredible potential for building a successful business. A unique and very useful book."

—Frank Heckman, President of Van Ede Heckman,
The Netherlands

"Dr. Ehin's *Unleashing Intellectual Capital* is thought provoking and enlightening. He built a compelling evolutionary argument demonstrating how hierarchical organizational structures stifle human social needs, thereby limiting organizational competitiveness. [Dr. Ehin] opened my eyes as to how an alternative structure, the shared access organization, affords modern organizations to compete in today's complex global society. Anyone planning to be a part of a successful 21st century enterprise should read his book and heed its advice on developing shared access organizations."

—Dr. Vicki R. Whiting, Assistant Professor, Vive and Bill Gore
School of Business, Westminster College

"*Unleashing Intellectual Capital* showcases Dr. Ehin's great breadth of knowledge, passion and intuitive reflection. This book provides the reader with deep personal insight necessary for the development of management theory. Ehin weaves corporate principles with human behavior resulting in a unique model which will bring success to any company in the Knowledge Age."

—Tom Lyons, Senior Adviser, Irish Productivity Center, Ireland

"Most pleasing about this work is the interdisciplinary approach to explaining management. Dr. Ehin's book redistributes the balance of power so that we can all see ourselves as innately-driven, and in search of personal fulfillment. Perhaps organizations will at this point be able to embrace sharing, openness and appreciate our capacities to learn, grow and self-organize as the keys to productivity. The argument in *Unleashing Intellectual Capital* should help us get back to some basic scientific truths about human behavior so that our organizations can all move forward, in a more honest and productive manner."

—**Stephen R. Baar**, Academic Vice President, Dean of Faculty,
Westminster College

"Dr. Ehin, a business professor and leader, weaves corporate principles with molecular biology, to reveal the many obstacles of what is considered 'traditional management.' Morality, responsibility and understanding are essential to not only the corporate world, but to the planet at large. This book will be an innovative tool for the corporate culture."

—**Jerry Kaufman**, Attorney-at-Law, Las Vegas, Nevada

"Dr. Charles Ehin makes a logical and interesting case for understanding human behavior in knowledge organizations by focusing on our biological and evolutionary development. He provides us with another way of building 'brain-rich' companies, who are the engines of progress and economic growth in modern society."

—**Anu Kaljurand**, Managing Director,
Baltic Management Conferences, Estonia

"*Unleashing Intellectual Capital* combines current management theory with important observations about human biology to create an organizational construct based on bio-logic. Professor Ehin brings these theories together with a model for creating a self-organizing learning organization that will be helpful in building and developing knowledge-age business."

—**Carl Lehmann**, CEO of RTW, and former President of the
Stored Value Group of American Express

"Organizations and individuals want a partnership where the individuals can use their ideas and skills and the organization will reward them for their contributions to the success of the business. Dr. Ehin is making a strong case that this movement is founded in recognizing and building on the positive aspects of our human nature. He has clearly explained why this is critical for satisfying the needs of both the business and the individual."

—John Giovale, Associate, W.L. Gore & Associates, Inc.

"This is excellent material. I found that many of the principles in the book were management concepts that I have been incorporating in my coaching career, which would indicate that his premise is right on track. I feel the information presented would help a wide variety of people tap into their potential, both professionally and personally."

—LaVell Edwards, Head Football Coach,
Brigham Young University

"Ehin's well written and accessible book draws the links between the evolutionary basis of behavior and the design and leadership of the knowledge-based enterprise. Finally a book that addresses the roots of human social behavior and the implications for organizations. Ehin links a fundamental insight with practical organizational implications. Well done!"

—Roderick White, Associate Professor, Richard Ivey School of
Business, The University of Western Ontario, Canada

UNLEASHING INTELLECTUAL CAPITAL

Unleashing Intellectual Capital

CHARLES EHIN, Ph.D.

Boston   Oxford   Auckland   Johannesburg   Melbourne   New Delhi

∞ Recognizing the importance of preserving what has been written, Butterworth–Heinemann prints its books on acid-free paper whenever possible.

 Butterworth–Heinemann supports the efforts of American Forests and the Global ReLeaf program in its campaign for the betterment of trees, forests, and our environment.

Library of Congress Cataloging-in-Publication Data
Ehin, Charles.
    Unleashing intellectual capital / by Charles Ehin.
        p.   cm.
    Includes bibliographical references and index.
    ISBN 0-7506-7246-3 (pbk. : alk. paper)
    1. Intellectual capital.   I. Title.

HD53.E37 2000
658.3'4--dc21   99-054446

British Library Cataloguing-in-Publication Data
A catalogue record for this book is available from the British Library.

The publisher offers special discounts on bulk orders of this book.
For information, please contact:

Manager of Special Sales
Butterworth–Heinemann
225 Wildwood Avenue
Woburn, MA 01801–2041
Tel: 781-904-2500
Fax: 781-904-2620

For information on all Butterworth–Heinemann publications available, contact our World Wide Web home page at: http://www.bh.com

10 9 8 7 6 5 4 3 2 1

Printed in the United States of America

To our grandchildren—Hollie, Matthew, Ryan, and Sarah

*May your generation encounter more
human-friendly and supportive social institutions
in your journeys through life.*

Contents

Figures

Foreword

It has been approximately 70 years since the Hawthorne studies were reported. These studies went against the grain of Taylorism, which provided the rationale for managing workers as if they were robots. In these 70 years, evidence grew for the fruition of the concepts about people and the organization of plants. Only recently have these ideas come to the consciousness of management, mainly because of the explosion of knowledge and the increasing value of people who possess knowledge.

Dr. Ehin goes further than most writers in exploring the reasons why management has to change from reliance on only the obvious need of workers for decent treatment as a means of motivation. He explores the other side of human nature, which is not avoidance behavior, but rather, the equally important need of workers to express their need for creativity.

Dr. Ehin has had tremendous experience in a variety of situations and, therefore, is unique in undertaking this task and relating it directly to present-day situations in the "knowledge time." His erudition to support his call for drastic changes in what he refers to as a transition from management to "unmanagement" is delightful to read when contrasted with the surface books on how to handle human relations. Beginning with A (anthropology) to Z (zoology), he reinforces his radical suggestions to management in traversing so large an area of human potential and its value.

This endeavor would seem pretentious, but the reader can see not pretension but scholarship, as evidenced by the bibliography that follows every chapter, right up to the time that Dr. Ehin started writing his book. The other accomplishments of this book are in covering such a wealth of material and the coherence of his arguments and suggestions. *Unleashing Intellectual Capital* is so well written that it is a delightful treat in management books.

As for me, having spent my life on similar issues covered in this book, I bow to Dr. Ehin.

Frederick Herzberg
Cummins Engine
Distinguished Professor Emeritus

Preface

As the former CEO of Hanover Insurance, Bill O'Brien, stipulated several years ago, "The ferment in management will continue until we find models that are more congruent with human nature." In this work, I present a management model that is exclusively based on the latest interdisciplinary evidence dealing with human nature.

Although this book is for everyone interested in developing and living in more "human-friendly," innovative, flexible, and productive organizations, I specifically wrote it for companies intent on maintaining a strategic edge in the next millennium through superior intellectual wealth management. Its purpose is threefold: First, to provide a fundamental understanding of what constitutes human nature, a subject currently lacking in management literature. Second, to show how this knowledge can be put to practical use in supporting voluntary collaborative behavior so vital for the creation of intellectual assets in the Knowledge Age. Third, to provide a general framework for generating, capturing, and leveraging intellectual capital.

I have found no magic formula or quick-fix for companies that have inimical learning capacities. Rather, by focusing on innate human drives, I offer fundamental measures to address root causes of social ills in various organizational settings and to identify environmental contexts that either foster or hinder the development of *voluntary* collaborative networks needed for knowledge production and application. Although the information contained within this book places an emphasis on management of corporations, the ideas put forth apply to any social institution interested in maximizing its social and intellectual capital.

By building on the most recent research in a variety of fields, such as anthropology, paleontology, molecular biology, neuroscience, evolutionary psychology, and sociobiology, I provide an exciting new biological perspective to the way we currently view organizations, and offer another step forward toward forming successful learning organizations in the Knowledge Age.

This book is the culmination of a long journey through uncharted waters for the past 25 years. The seeds for the venture, however, I believe were cast decades before and after the end of World War II in war-torn central Europe by two very caring elementary schoolteachers. Both had returned home from prisoner-of-war camps with scarred bodies but unbroken spirits. Never before or since have I encountered such compassionate teachers who loved their work and their students. They taught me at an early age that knowledge was much more than facts and figures. Essentially, they taught that knowledge was the essence of life itself. What they planted in my mind has made it easier for me to grasp the paradigm shifts taking place today and made me keenly aware of the importance of human nature in the new discontinuous world environment. I am very grateful to those two gracious gentlemen for having provided me with a sense of self-direction and an appreciation for the power of unhindered inquiry and dialogue.

Charles Ehin
July 1999

Acknowledgments

I am extremely grateful to several people for making this endeavor possible. Sylvia Sullivant provided me with unbelievably speedy and errorless word processing support. Without her enthusiasm and dedication, I would probably still be writing the original draft of this book. Unfortunately, she left Salt Lake City before its completion.

One of my graduates in organizational behavior, molecular biologist Dr. Michael Glass, provided me with valuable suggestions as I began working on the book. His advice was very beneficial from a biological perspective. My dear friend, Dr. Susan Gardner, helped me make the first draft of the manuscript readable in addition to imparting "tons" of encouragement and prized recommendations. I have a hard time imagining completing the book without her initial support.

Tonya Purdie always greeted me with a big smile and a "no problem" attitude as I kept running to her unexpectedly to ask for help with innumerable additions and changes to the manuscript. She was also an absolute wizard with computer network problems and solutions. Carl Champagne, President and CEO of Data Systems International and a long-time friend, constantly reminded me that persistence is the secret to every successful venture. He also provided two examples from his extensive business experience for the book. Karen Speerstra, the Publishing Director, and Rita Lombard, the Assistant Editor for Butterworth–Heinemann, provided invaluable suggestions and support at the end as I polished the final draft for publication.

Last, but not least, my wife Betty made sure that I touched terra firma after my periodic "intergalactic travels" in quest of new perspectives. Besides providing needed realism for my ideas and editing all my drafts, she also unselfishly made sure that I had plenty of uninterrupted time to place my thoughts on paper. She has been my guiding light for more than 40 years.

Introduction:
Time for Unmanagement

*Courage is not simply one of the virtues, but the
form of every virtue at the testing point.*
C. S. Lewis, *The Screwtape Letters*

Increasing intellectual capital cannot be *managed* in the traditional
sense. Therefore, *Unleashing Intellectual Capital* is not another book
about how to "manage" knowledge in our organizations with all
sorts of new-age technologies and associated elaborate methodologies, although intellectual capital creation is one of its major themes.
Its intent is also not to prescribe another novel way to manage people
in our collective endeavors, although the development of highly sustained levels of social capital is the other principle topic of the work.
Rather, this book is about the power of "unmanagement." It is
grounded on the *inherent* genetic tendencies of human beings, which
have so far been almost totally ignored by business and our other social institutions. Thus, the work is based on common sense that, regrettably, seems to be quite uncommon at times.

We are all aware that hundreds of millions of dollars can be
saved by companies with the development and use of advanced processes and technologies. Those dollars can also be wasted, as we wit-
nessed in the overzealous drive to automate processes in the automo-
bile industry in the 1980s, and in the unthinking reengineering that
drove much of the *Fortune 500*'s present and future talent to the new
.Com 500 that is now coming to the fore. Innovation still provides the
best means to increase profit margins, however, through the creation
of leading-edge products and services. Yet, before any organization

aspires to generate highly sustained levels of intellectual capital for competitive advantage, it must first gain a thorough understanding of what constitutes human nature. Essentially, we need to fully grasp who we are before we can develop appropriate social settings capable of leveraging the creative and innovative potential contained within all of us.

Success in the Knowledge Age demands that we have the fore-sight and courage to let go of the Newtonian clockwork or machine metaphor on which most of our organizations are still founded and embrace the logic of the biological and quantum physics world based on the principles of self-organization or unmanagement. After all, we humans are (at least by the latest account that I am aware of) *fully* developed biological beings functioning 24 hours a day in a self-organizing mode down to the level of individual molecules. Therefore, managing humans makes little sense, even if it was actually possible. Unmanagement is clearly a much more appropriate option.

Beginning with the dawn of agriculture and extending through the Industrial Age, civilizations *may* have been well served by control and dissemination of explicit knowledge—facts, instructions, rules, and procedures—by the privileged few. In the Knowledge Age, however, societies are primarily dependent on tacit knowledge—expertise, reasoning, judgment, and insight. As a result, organizations that once prospered or failed on the basis of machine and muscle power now can only succeed or vanish on the basis of collective brain power—the extent to which they can attain *voluntary* collaboration among their members, permitting the selfless sharing of ideas, thus making tacit knowledge explicit for competitive advantage. Again, we must remember that knowledge, especially tacit knowledge, cannot be forced or supervised out of people.

The first and most critical step toward making this knowledge happen is to accommodate the vital role of human nature in organizational life. We all come into this world with both innate self-centered drives (e.g., concern for control, rank, status, territory, possessions) and other-centered innate drives (e.g., concern for attachment, affiliation, altruism, care-giving, care-receiving). Unfortunately, most current organizations with their prevailing top-down, command-and-control administrative systems are unknowingly mainly impacting their people's self-centered drives. At the same time, their leaders are asking these people to be good team players and committed to institutional goals. Obviously, this style is not an effective way to run knowledge-intensive businesses where the exchange of tacit knowledge is the key to success and, therefore, the other-centered drives need to have an opportunity to be expressed.

We must keep in mind that we have the capacity to be both the most savage creatures on Earth, as well as the most compassionate. Having survived World War II as a refugee and a displaced person, I can vividly attest to these two inherent human qualities. I believe the major determining factor as to which side of our genetic makeup is expressed more than the other (in normal people) is the environmental context in which individuals find themselves. Consequently, if organizations are serious about increasing their knowledge assets to achieve increased competitiveness, they must first place primary emphasis on developing a solid social capital base. That is, they must create a social foundation that will facilitate the *balanced* expression of both sides of human nature necessary before voluntary sharing of tacit knowledge can take place. Thus, the rudimentary goal of organizations should be to try to narrow the differences between our unchanging human nature and the demands of the work context.

Accordingly, the purpose of *Unleashing Intellectual Capital* is threefold: First, to provide a fundamental interdisciplinary understanding of human nature, a subject currently lacking in organizational literature. Second, to show how this knowledge of human nature can be put to practical use in developing highly sustained levels of voluntary collaborative behavior, which is indispensable for the creation of knowledge assets in the third millennium. Finally, to render a comprehensive framework for generating, capturing, and leveraging intellectual capital founded on the balanced expression of our innate drives. In order to achieve that end, I have included short business examples and summarized key organizational considerations at the end of each chapter for those readers who may get a little "queasy" when confronted, at times, with extensive interdisciplinary theoretical deliberations.

Although the information contained within this book places an emphasis on the conduct of business firms, the ideas put forth apply equally to any organization interested in maximizing its social and intellectual capital. For instance, I believe that all educational institutions, from kindergarten to colleges and universities, can benefit from this work both from an academic as well as a societal perspective.

1

The Competitive Advantage

Knowledge is the frontier of tomorrow.
Denis Waitley, *Seeds of Greatness*

Gaining and maintaining a leadership position in a fast-paced, global environment requires companies to adapt a deliberate strategy for creating, developing, and applying knowledge. The reason for this need is straightforward. At an ever-accelerating rate, the value of products and services comes less from the tangibles of material resources and physical labor and more from the intangibles of exceptional intellectual wealth- and knowledge-producing processes. In addition, innovative ideas cannot be supervised or forced out of people.

Consequently, organizations in the Knowledge Age need a new management model for generating, capturing, and leveraging intellectual assets in order to stay competitive. In *Unleashing Intellectual Capital,* I describe the fundamental tenets required for developing a comprehensive system for creating and applying highly sustained levels of intellectual capital in the new millennium.

THE HIERARCHY

What is the most relevant model for organizational success in the Knowledge Age? It definitely cannot be found by following the current norm. Surrounded by a world of constantly increasing change, uncertainty, and complexity, managing even with "modernized" standard strategies would be tantamount to purchasing a one-way ticket to the final resting place of defunct enterprises.

What, then, is today's management norm, and why should we abandon it? Few people would disagree that most organizations are governed by some form of top-down hierarchy, no matter how much lip service may be given to the present vogue of total quality management (TQM) and self-directed teams. Worship of the hierarchy and its corresponding machine-logic has been especially apparent since the beginning of the Industrial Revolution approximately 300 years ago. In fact, the command-and-control paradigm has been and still continues to be so pervasive that many people are convinced we have no other alternative. Fortunately, lack of choice is not the case.

The problem with a hierarchy is that it is founded on two counterproductive assertions that also serve as the basis for its advocacy. The first premise suggests that hierarchies are a natural phenomenon and, therefore, unavoidable. This premise is true *only* if we prefer to rely primarily on the most primitive drives of the lowest level of our three-tiered brain—the reptilian complex—which evolved approximately half a billion years ago. According to MacLean (1973), a highly recognized neuroscientist, this complex plays a key role in territoriality, aggressive behavior, and development of hierarchies and rituals. These features equate to the intelligence of a reptile. As the late Carl Sagan (1977) put it:

> Despite occasional welcome exceptions, this seems to me to characterize a great deal of modern human bureaucratic and political behavior. I do not mean that the neocortex is not functioning at all in an American political convention . . . But it is striking how much of our actual behavior—as distinguished from what we say and think about it—can be described in reptilian terms.

If we believe humans are much more intelligent than reptiles, it would make more sense to rely on our characteristically human social side, a part of our nature that evolved much more recently and that is especially pertinent regarding creativity and innovation.

The second assertion supporting the hierarchical model is grounded in the belief that social organizations should be structured in accordance to a mechanistic or machine model. That is, organizations should be developed and run like well-oiled machines. This philosophy was initiated by engineers and economists during the Industrial Revolution. The problem with this premise is that it confuses control with order. People are not machines in any shape or form; therefore, we must change the way we think about all our social institutions, particularly knowledge-intensive organizations.

Machines need to be monitored, controlled, and maintained by external sources (although that is changing with the introduction of software such as fuzzy-logic). People and organizations, however, are living systems, not machines. Living systems have the innate capacity to self-assemble, self-sustain, change constantly, reproduce, learn, and self-organize. They are able to create order out of any situation without external controls. As culture expert Lisa Hoecklin (1995) maintains, "People within organizations do not simply react to their environment as a ship to waves. They actively select, interpret, and create their environment."

Further, as we are discovering today, externally imposed controls on complex biological systems (such as people), even through pay-for-performance plans, actually produce unpredictable and severe negative consequences rather than the desired order. As noted rewards expert Alfie Kohn (1998) maintains, "The fact that people don't enjoy being controlled, even if they need or want money, helps understand why those tactics [using money to manipulate people] inevitably backfire." Instead, he continues, "We need to meet with individuals and treat them as learners to be engaged and potential decision-makers, rather than as pets to be trained and recognized."

Almost two decades ago, William Ouchi (1981) made an interesting observation: "Social organizations are incompatible with formality, distance, and contractualism. They proceed smoothly only with intimacy, subtlety, and trust." His comments remind us that we need to become more comfortable using *bio-logic* (I borrowed the term "bio-logic" from Kevin Kelly, author of *Out of Control*) instead of continuing to rely primarily on machine-logic in running our social institutions. As we know from experience, biological systems are extremely adaptable, resilient to adversity, and capable of constant novelty. Thus, it behooves us to focus more on the strength of natural systems and design organizations that encompass their basic principles. Essentially, the goal should be to develop social arrangements without the need for imposed structure, where coordination is voluntarily achieved without control.

Still, organizations look around every corner to anticipate the next "Messiah," using guises such as TQM, reengineering, empowerment, and teams. Sadly, the followers of these new "commandments" have been disappointed. Rather than experiencing increased productivity, many institutions continue to encounter inflexibility, indolence, greed, inefficiency, and even violence among their employees. Teamsters' Union Communications Director Matt Witt (1998) made an interesting observation in a recent newspaper article entitled, "End of an Era in Workplace Cooperation Experiments." In summing up what he thinks has been wrong with these participative programs, Witt comments: "The main reason many of the new 'cooperative' programs fail after an initial honeymoon is that workers discover that the basic premise is false. Despite the 'win-win' rhetoric, a conflict remains between the interests of workers and the interests of management that cannot be papered over or wished away."

People are not simply a means of production. They are biological systems constantly seeking to fulfill their needs and aspirations. Consequently, cooperative endeavors can only be maximized and sustained when individual and organizational goals overlap. This process is not magical. Even from an economics perspective, people in companies are not assets, but investors, similar to shareholders. Shareholders invest their money in an institution, whereas members of a firm invest their time, energy, and intellect. For this reason, they should be considered associates or partners instead of expendable parts of a machine or "employees."

After all, we join organizations in order to make a living (survive) more productively than by working alone. Thus, the ultimate purpose and vision of a social entity should coincide, to a considerable degree, with those of its members. Otherwise, little *voluntary* collaboration is possible in a social entity other than among small informal quasi-clandestine groups of people who band together for mutual support in what they perceive to be a win-lose instead of a win-win environment.

The main problem is that few people have ever experienced anything other than top-down structures and, therefore, are not willing to let go of the "security blanket" of a hierarchy model no matter where they are situated in an organization. Even knowledgeable leaders who seem to know their efforts will be relatively futile keep investing valuable time, energy, and resources in order to keep "streamlining" hierarchies. A habit that is centuries old is extremely hard to break.

SOCIAL CAPITAL

Fortunately, leading practitioners and theoreticians from around the world are beginning to reach consensus that business success in the Knowledge Age depends primarily on the capacity to generate knowledge assets—or intellectual capital—and to expeditiously get those innovations in the hands of global customers. Conversely, most people have yet to realize that high levels of intellectual capital can be generated only by intense voluntary collaboration among all members of an organization and its allies. This voluntary collaborative behavior, also known as *social capital*, permits the inherent creative potential of all individuals to be unleashed, shared, and applied. In other words, without a proper social context, intellectual capital is hard to come by.

Thus, voluntary collaboration provides the primary basis for sustainable competitive advantage in a knowledge society. On the surface, this advantage appears simple, but in reality, it is extremely difficult to achieve. Essentially, highly developed collaborative relationships are self-sustaining and mutually reinforcing. Such relationships take a long time to foster and, therefore, are almost impossible to duplicate by other firms, unlike the duplication of new technologies, software, and other discrete procedures or methods. *Fortune* magazine Editorial Director Geoffrey Colvin (1997), for instance, makes it clear that people are now becoming our most important resource. He states: "Bottom line: the more that infotech revolutionizes business, the more economically valuable are the exclusively human qualities of the people who work in companies."

Another feature of social capital that makes it difficult to imitate is the impossibility of demanding it or effecting it by increased monetary rewards. Genuine relationships can only be founded in a social context that has high levels of *trust* and *altruism*. Unfortunately, these qualities are rare commodities in most organizations where, instead, competitive positioning and power over subordinates is the order of the day. Competitiveness is severely counterproductive in an age of knowledge, as accurately portrayed by Kim and Mauborgne (1997). "Unlike the traditional factors of production—land, labor, and capital—knowledge is a resource locked in the human mind. Creating and sharing knowledge are intangible activities that can neither be supervised nor forced out of people. They happen only when people cooperate voluntarily."

We need to let go of the hierarchical machine model. That model may have served its purpose in the past in controlling the activities of large institutions employing large numbers of relatively uneducated workers and new immigrants while operating in a relatively stable nonglobal environment; however, we must move on with developing and using a totally different philosophy for the future. We need to realize that it makes absolutely no sense to deal with living systems like machines if we want to develop organizations that can change continuously and fully access the intelligence of their members.

Concepts such as TQM, empowerment, or teams do have value. They are worthy of consideration, but in the traditional environment these concepts eventually fall victim to the hierarchy. Leaders of the future need to look beyond individual programs at something much more fundamental, integrative, and easily understood. That "something" should be a natural phenomenon—bio-logic—whose principles are based neither on the most primitive animal instincts nor on an artificially contrived mechanistic control model.

GENETIC TENDENCIES

If we agree that bio-logic is much more appropriate than machine-logic as a fundamental metaphor for organizational success in the Knowledge Age, then what aspects of the human biological system do we need to concentrate on first? I believe emphatically that our primary focus needs to be on understanding human nature and its link to voluntary collaborative behavior so vital for nurturing creativity and innovation. Essentially, we need to develop and sustain organizational constructs that are more congruent with human nature and not with machines.

Much has been insinuated and assumed about human nature up to the present. Unfortunately, no management source specifically deals with human nature and how different organizational contexts affect the duality of our innate (but by no means hard-wired) drives. Therefore, relying on the latest interdisciplinary research conducted in diverse fields such as anthropology, paleontology, evolutionary psychology, molecular biology, neuroscience, and sociobiology, I have attempted to fill the void with this book.

At the outset, we need to distinguish between instincts and innate human drives. We blink when something flashes by our eyes. We are startled by a sudden and unexpected loud noise. These reactions are automatic or instinctive responses to the sudden changes in our environment. With innate drives, however, we have a choice in how we express or fail to activate our reactions. Our sex drives and our need for affiliation are good examples. We all possess these innate drives to some degree, yet how we carry them out or choose not to express them at all depends on our genetic makeup and how we perceive a given environmental context. The distinction between instincts and innate drives becomes progressively clearer in the chapters that follow.

I am convinced that "unmanagement"—that fostering of human nature that leads to voluntary collaboration—will provide the competitive advantage to organizations that intend to prosper in the twenty-first century and beyond. Hence, emphasis should be shifted from controlling organizational behavior to nurturing positive *emergent* behavior or self-organization. After all, humans have evolved to function as social creatures more than any other species of which we are aware.

As I alluded previously, although it may not be apparent, self-organization or emergent behavior takes place even in companies that employ the tightest forms of top-down control and in prisoner-of-war camps. The Hawthorne Studies at the Western Electric Company in Chicago in the late 1920s and early 1930s first made this observation from a management perspective. The initial inquiry into the relationship between workplace illumination and employee productivity soon turned into the first extensive social behavior studies. One of the discoveries was that informal organizations (self-organization) run parallel to formal structures and are unavoidable. As Peter Senge (1998) noted, "Everyone knows that no work ever gets done by following rules. It gets done through the informal network." I do not believe that there is anyone who has had some work experience who cannot identify with this statement.

Thus, the type of organizational context in which people find themselves largely affects how emergent behavior plays itself out. In an increasingly volatile and complex global environment, it makes much more sense to attempt to support "overt" positive self-organizing efforts (voluntary collaboration) than to waste energy attempting to force structure and control on all forms of social behavior that ultimately facilitate "covert" collaborative efforts that seldom fully support formal organizational goals.

EVOLUTION AND THE FUTURE

My conviction is based on the study of the human evolutionary past, as well as the predictions of futurists for the year 2020 and beyond. Ironically, a look in both directions provides similar conclusions. For example, beginning with the origins of life approximately 3.5 billion years ago, the evolutionary process has produced increasingly complex life forms in an "unmanaged" setting. That is, organisms have become more complex not according to a "master plan" but by means of constant interaction and mutually beneficial adjustments. Self-organization, natural selection, and chance have been the fundamental forces for the development of early single-celled organisms to human beings.

From an historical perspective, modern humans (and their predecessors for millions of years before) have lived roughly 98 percent of their existence as a species in small hunting-and-gathering bands held loosely together by informal networks and without the services of a single chief. Our innate human drives have evolved in this type of an environment, and these genetically determined behavior patterns have not changed in the past 200 thousand years. Inherently, we lived in societies governed by the principles of self-organization. Only since the advent of agriculture and the domestication of animals have we developed more mechanistic and nonorganic forms of social interaction. As a result, the gap between our unchanging human nature and our self-imposed changing environment has continued to widen until today. That gap must be narrowed if we want to generate highly *sustained* levels of social and intellectual capital.

What is ahead in the next 20 to 30 years? Futurists suggest that socially we will complete evolving from an industrial to a knowledge society and thus large, cumbersome organizations will be replaced by small enterprises connected through virtual networks. In other words, the current era marks the beginning of the end for "big." Longer life spans will place greater emphasis on wisdom and community support rather than on status and upward mobility. Further, evidence suggests that Generation Xers are rebelling against corporate greed and materialism and are promoting social responsibility, quality of life, and a greener environment. It appears these young people have a greater purpose in life than simply economic gain.

In addition, shortages of skilled labor will dictate that a premium be placed on treating people well and respecting their desire for personal growth. Globally, a larger worldwide middle class will evolve, women will gain greater prominence, and more focus will be placed on peace and prosperity for people everywhere.

These changes point out that an increasing number of knowledge workers around the world will carry their own means of production with them; that is, between their ears. Increasing the importance of the mind and the innovative intangible ideas that originate from it will create a need for more cooperation. Hence, organizations and individuals will need to work together as *partners*, sharing their fruits of labor equitably because the production of intellectual assets depends primarily on voluntary relationships instead of competition. Peter Drucker (1999), probably the greatest management authority and the most prolific business writer of the twentieth century, makes this point quite clear in a recent article:

> Increasingly, performance in these knowledge-based industries will come to depend on running the institution so as to attract, hold, and motivate knowledge workers. When this

can no longer be done by satisfying knowledge workers' greed, as we are now trying to do, it will have to be done by satisfying their values, and by giving them social recognition and social power. It will have to be done by turning them from subordinates into fellow executives, and from employees, however well paid, into partners.

Accordingly, labor will be capital, not cost. Out of necessity, therefore, an inordinate need to know how to influence positive emergent behavior instead of trying to find more effective ways to control employees will take center stage. Fostering human nature in a balanced fashion will become the primary ingredient for organizational success.

NOT A UTOPIAN FANTASY

In the multidisciplinary fields previously cited, much headway has been made in the past two decades in determining the functions of the mind and human nature. We now need to apply these new discoveries to our social institutions to make them more "human friendly," flexible, and productive. As suggested before, people—not technology—will provide the only sustainable competitive advantage to organizations in the future.

In case you are becoming squeamish, I want to assure you that this book is not about a utopian fantasy suggesting the return to a distant paradise lost. I do cite anthropological evidence dealing with the life of our distant hunter-gatherer ancestors (as do evolutionary psychologists and others), but only to show how our innate drives developed over millions of years of evolution. However, in no way do I insinuate turning back the clock—an impossible and unwarranted idea.

What I am advocating is the *practical* application of the latest knowledge about human nature in business and other social settings. Unknowingly, most firms today rely primarily on people's selfish innate drives to carry out day-to-day activities, while concurrently asking these people to be good team players. That request is like swimming against a strong current to get across a river instead of going with the flow. I believe nurturing both sides (the self-centered and the community-centered sides) of human nature produces much more desirable outcomes. A nurturing environment increases the quality of life within an institution. It also increases creativity, flexibility, and the ability to leverage knowledge as a competitive advantage.

Despite these assertions, this book was not written to offer a step-by-step process to heal ailing organizations. In fact, I believe that no precise step-by-step process can address all the intricacies of a social collective. If only one lesson is retained from this venture, it should be that an organization is an extremely complex entity that cannot be "fixed" with simple measures. As is the case in most situations, the quick-fix usually focuses only on the symptoms and not the fundamental causes. I hope to address root causes and to identify environments that foster positive emergent behavior, or social capital, in response to innate human drives that, in turn, will lead to the development of increased and more sustainable levels of intellectual capital. Hence, the paramount theme of the book is that without first cultivating sufficiently high levels of voluntary collaboration by fostering the *totality* of human nature, organizations will have little chance of propagating the necessary intellectual assets to stay competitive in the Knowledge Age.

Clearly, every organization must make a profit to survive. Ironically, however, increasing numbers of studies show that enterprises that focus exclusively on the bottom line are in fact much less profitable than firms that place a primary emphasis on the people part of the equation. Therefore, I submit that those businesses that are more nimble in grasping the importance of understanding and applying human nature will lead the pack in years to come. As suggested by Thomas Petzinger (1997) of *The Wall Street Journal*, "The new model for organizations is the biological world, where uncontrolled actions produce stunningly efficient and robust results, all through adaptation and self-organization." Most people still fail to grasp the importance of the biological model in our increasingly discontinuous environment. However, Colvin (1997) states:

> There is no avoiding it. The external search for sustainable competitive advantage is leading us straight into the squishy softness of culture and character. Many business people

won't like it. They won't be comfortable talking with colleagues about trust, honesty, purpose, values, and other topics out of the self-help section of the bookstore. They will have to face the fact that they will likely be eaten alive by competitors who confront these issues with relish.

AN OVERVIEW

In the next two chapters, I introduce and summarize some of the interdisciplinary foundations pertaining to innate human drives and emergent behavior. Next, I show how human nature plays itself out in two diametrically opposite resource management environments. Subsequently, four general tenets are presented for fostering community-centered behavior or social capital. These tenets are not meant as how-to steps because the elements of each situation are different. Consequently, I do not suggest control, manipulation, and *precise* procedures either, for these elements cannot be part of the self-organizing perspective. I then discuss certain key options that need to be considered in developing and running social organizations where authentic collaborative behavior is emphasized in the pursuit of knowledge assets. I conclude by presenting a comprehensive framework for generating, capturing, and leveraging intellectual capital.

We have entered an era where knowledge is the primary source for wealth creation. What needs to be realized is that our transition from the Industrial Age (where we were constantly in hot pursuit of predictability and control or machine-logic) to this new epoch is just as gut wrenching as the metamorphosis experienced by those who left the Agricultural Age behind. We now need to become comfortable with perpetual change, uncertainty, and complexity of our own making. Such solace requires an in-depth understanding of our evolved human qualities and the quest of serendipitous self-organizing systems or bio-logic. People and organizations who grasp this fact more quickly will be in a better position to maximize their knowledge-generation capabilities in the years to come.

AN EXAMPLE

Participative management, prescribed as the ultimate "medicine" for healing whatever ails a hierarchical organization, has come in various shapes and forms for the past four decades. Let me refresh your memory with a partial list of participative management concepts in case you have forgotten. They are as follows in a "rough" chronological order:

> Quality of Work Life (QWL)
> Job Enrichment
> Quality Circles
> Teams
> Total Quality Management (TQM)
> Empowerment
> Learning Organizations

Have organizations had success with the implementation of any of these management methodologies? Yes. More projects have been implemented satisfactorily than have failed. Regrettably, based on my experience and studies, most of the successful initiatives have been left to "die on the vine" after some initial short-term positive results. Before I divulge why I believe such a large failure rate has occurred, I will first present an example of one of the participative management projects with which I was involved.

As is well known, Job Enrichment was the brainchild of Frederick Herzberg, the world-renowned motivation expert. Very briefly, Job Enrichment is based on Herzberg's two-factor theory of motivation, which stipulates that two continuums instead of one are present in understanding motivation. That is, no one continuum exists, with job satisfaction at one end of the scale and job dissatisfaction at the other end. Rather, two continuums are necessary, with one showing low-to-high job dissatisfaction (the hygiene factors) and the other showing low-to-high job satisfaction (the motivation factors). The hygiene factors include:

> Job security
> Pay
> Working conditions

Interpersonal relations
Supervision
Fringe benefits
Company policies

Herzberg believes that the hygiene factors have nothing to do with motivation. These dissatisfiers simply have to be adequately addressed if for no other reason than out of courtesy and fairness to organizational members; hence the name, hygiene factors. Conversely, motivators include:

Achievement
Meaningful work
Responsibility
Growth and advancement
Recognition

For true motivation (based on intrinsic elements) to occur, the motivators need to be built into an individual's job. That goal is accomplished by what Herzberg calls *horizontal and vertical loading*. That is, horizontally, an attempt is made to give an individual a complete module of a process to work on instead of a meaningless "slice" as on an assembly line. Vertically, more responsibility and recognition are included in a job by taking some of the responsibility away from an individual's immediate supervisor.

In the mid-1970s, the Air Force Logistics Command decided to contract Herzberg to assist with Job Enrichment efforts throughout the command. Hill Air Force Base near Ogden, Utah, was chosen to be the initial "pilot" Logistics Center where the program was to be introduced before the other four major centers would initiate their own projects. I was selected to head the Hill Program on the Air Force side, probably because I had a Ph.D. in business administration, which "obviously" superbly qualified me for the job! Consequently, I had the opportunity to work directly with Fred Herzberg. He and I became good friends, and I admire him to this day for his contributions to management.

Briefly, I learned a lot from Herzberg and through my involvement with the Hill Job Enrichment program. It was a challenge, but I had fun in the process along with some very dedicated people with whom I had the pleasure of working. As a result, we were successful in implementing Job Enrichment projects throughout the Logistics Center that resulted in considerable cost savings for the Logistics Command. Many of the results were gained by unsophisticated means. In one instance, by simply including the name and telephone number of the person who had refurbished a component, a high level of responsibility was built into the job. The worker now not only accepted greater responsibility for the repair of the item but also received direct feedback from around the world without that information first being screened by his or her boss. We were even able to enrich some janitorial jobs by making the people involved responsible for managing their own supplies and schedules.

In 1979, after being evacuated out of Tehran, Iran, I was put in charge of the Office of Productivity at the Logistics Command Headquarters in Dayton, Ohio. I was now responsible for all the productivity enhancement efforts throughout the Command. I soon discovered that the program at Hill Air Force Base was losing its momentum and effectiveness through no fault of the people who were still running it. Management had simply lost interest, and there now were "new" programs to be advocated. In addition, our efforts to implement Job Enrichment at the other Logistics Centers had run head-on into the "not-invented-here syndrome." Finally, Herzberg had refused to extend his contract because of changes in command at several of the Logistics Centers.

Why such an unforeseen ending to what seemed to be a beneficial program from both the motivational and cost savings perspectives? The answer is relatively simple. Long-term change is impossible to effect without changing how the entire system functions. If you want people to accept more responsibility for their jobs and activities of the entire organization, the context surrounding their jobs must also change. As I stated before, people naturally self-organize around any situation. Thus, if the hierarchical structure remains in place, everyone knows what he or she must do to be successful in such an environment. Individuals must continue to "climb the ladder" or be faced with a dead-end job. Of course, working one's way up the pyramid takes considerable time and energy, leaving little enthusiasm for Job Enrichment or any other programs that are not key to an individual's survival.

KEY CONSIDERATIONS

- Hierarchies are not a natural phenomenon unless we want to rely almost exclusively on the most primitive drives of our reptilian complex.
- People are biological entities and not machines by any stretch of the imagination. Therefore, we need to grasp the difference between control and order. Machines need to have external control mechanisms. People naturally self-organize around a situation or an opportunity, thus establishing situation-specific order.
- Organizational members are investors similar to venture capitalists, except they invest their time, energy, and knowledge instead of exclusively money. Hence, if you treat people as a cost or expendable resource, they will respond differently than if you treat them as partners capable of learning continuously and making responsible decisions.
- You cannot circumvent human nature. Consequently, by understanding our inherent genetic predispositions, we can narrow the gap between our unchanging human nature and the organizational context rather than unknowingly widening it. Those companies that are able to close that gap will have competitive advantage in the Knowledge Age.

REFERENCES

Colvin, G. (1997) "The Changing Act of Becoming Unbeatable," *Fortune*, November 24, pp. 299–300.

Drucker, P.F. (1999) "Beyond the Information Revolution," *The Atlantic Monthly*, October, pp. 47–57.

Hoecklin, L. (1995) *Managing Cultural Differences*. Addison-Wesley, New York, NY, p. 10.

Kelly, K. (1994) *Out of Control: The Rise of Neo-biological Civilization*. William Patrick Books, Addison-Wesley, New York, NY, p. 2.

Kim, C. and Mauborgne, R. (1997) "Fair Process: Managing in the Knowledge Economy," *Harvard Business Review*, July–August, pp. 65–75.

Kohn, A. (1998) "How Incentives Undermine Performance," *The Journal for Quality and Participation*, March–April, pp. 7–13.

MacLean, P.D. (1973) *A Triune Concept of the Brain Behavior*. University of Toronto Press, Toronto, Canada, pp. 6–22.

Ouchi, W. (1981) *Theory Z*. Avon Books, New York, NY, p. 79.

Petzinger, T., Jr. (1997) "Self-Organization Will Free Employees to Act Like Bosses," *Wall Street Journal*, January 3, p. 31.

Sagan, C. (1977) *The Dragons of Eden*. Random House, New York, NY, pp. 60–61.

Senge, P. (1998) "Teaching an Organization to Learn," *News for a Change* (Published by the Association for Quality and Participation), March, pp. 1, 9.

Witt, M. (1998) "End of an Era in Workplace Cooperation Experiments," *The Salt Lake Tribune*, April 24, p. A19.

<u>2</u>

The Critical Elements

We are never prepared for what we expect.
James H. Michener, *Caravans*

Understanding who we are as human beings is key to developing organizational constructs based on bio-logic. What is our primary purpose in life? What is our evolutionary history? Are we born with certain general predispositions or are we born with a blank mind that is subsequently molded by the environment? The answers to these questions help us understand human nature in a much more intimate way.

WHO ARE WE?

Our kind has reached its present state after three and a half billion years of biological evolution on Earth. The progression has not been in accordance with a master plan but by chance, natural selection, and self-organization in relationship to our immediate environment. Consequently, all living things from bacteria to modern humans, or *Homo sapiens*, have some aspects in common. Concurrently, every member of a species is unique and without an exact equal. For instance, approximately 60 billion people have been born on this planet since the dawn of modern humans. Out of all this mass of humanity, however, no two individuals have ever been identical, nor will that situation happen in the future. As reported by Richard Monastersky

(1998) of *National Geographic*, biochemist Gerald Joyce of the San Diego Scripps Research Institute defines any form of life as "a self-sustained chemical system capable of undergoing Darwinian evolution." Hence, life in general at both the individual and collective levels centers primarily around the attainment and management of scarce resources for the sake of survival and the perpetuation of the species.

By no means does this line of reasoning insinuate that we fundamentally live in a "dog-eat-dog" world. On the contrary, Darwinian evolutionary principles are not solely based on the notion of survival of the fittest or natural selection. This theory is only one part of the equation. If survival of the fittest was the only factor in the evolutionary process, life as we know it would probably have disappeared from our planet long ago with the last member of the last surviving species shouting from the mountain top, "I won! I won!" Instead, life is much more complex than such a notion for several reasons.

First, biological systems are not continuously evolving as many people still believe. Evolution takes place more in stages or in accordance with the law of punctuated equilibrium as Niles Eldredge and Stephen Gould (1972), two distinguished biologists, first proposed in the early 1970s. That is, a particular species evolves to a certain level and then remains stable for a considerable period in which little change occurs. The organism may then develop a branch or branches of similar breeds, or disappear altogether. Modern humans, for example, have not changed anatomically in approximately the past 200 thousand years. In the meantime, we have proliferated cultures, become capable of changing our environment, and in the process, forgotten our ancient hunter-gatherer origins. We may yet turn out to be our own worst enemies.

Second, living things depend on serendipitous and symbiotic relationships or self-organization for their survival. All we have to do is visit a meadow or forest and observe nature in action to grasp this phenomenon. No "CEO" directs plants where and how to grow or tells insects or birds which areas they should inhabit. Trying to control biological systems often produces unknown detrimental effects, as exemplified by numerous attempts by humans to manage wilderness and wildlife. In observing nature, what becomes immediately obvious is that living systems from tiny insects to giant trees are closely interdependent. Reciprocity reigns, not mortal combat. Thus, we also have the innate capacity for constant learning, an insatiable appetite for novelty, and the need to interact with others. This essential reciprocity may explain why we seek comfort in nonadversarial social relationships instead of "winner-take-all" situations.

In *The Origin of Species,* Charles Darwin (1936) suggested that pressure from the appearance of new forms of life produces gradual extinction of older, less adaptive species. He stated "that as new species in the course of time are formed through natural selection, others will become rarer and rarer, and finally extinct. The forms which stand in closest competition with those undergoing modification and improvement will naturally suffer most."

Statistical paleontologist David Raup (1991) of the University of Chicago is convinced that population pressures from new species have little to do with extinction. He believes that bad luck instead of bad genes causes most extinctions, and that the most likely cause for mass extinctions among the most serious candidates considered is meteorite impact. "Only large impacts have the required energy, are known to have occurred often enough to do the job, yet are rare enough to thwart adaptation by natural selection."

Well-known paleobiologist and writer Stephen Gould (1993) fully supports Raup's theory. In *Eight Little Piggies*, he convincingly argues that the "directional trends produced by wedging [Darwin's metaphor for new species pressures] do occur, but they scarcely cry for recognition from every quarry and hilltop. The overwhelming majority of paleontological trends tell no obvious story of conquest in competition. . . . A species can only evolve for current benefits and deliver its future fate to the wheel of fortune." The wheel of fortune rests mostly at the mercy of comets and asteroids.

Clearly, as I mentioned previously, no apparent master plan exists for the past, present, and future evolutionary cycles. Stephen Gould (1996) makes this point quite clear in *Full House*:

> Wind back the tape of life to the origin of modern multicellular animals in the Cambrian explosion, let the tape play again from this identical starting point and the replay will populate the earth . . . with a radically different set of creatures. The chance that this alternative set will contain anything remotely like a human being must be effectively nil,

while the probability of any kind of creature endowed with self-consciousness must also be extremely small.

Again, chance, natural selection, and self-organization determine our fate instead of a predetermined path to increased complexity and perfection.

We need to be aware of one more important factor about ourselves before we begin to look at more specific details of human nature. Even though behavioral genetics is still in its infancy, new research overwhelmingly indicates that people are not born with a brain that is a "clean slate" waiting to be filled by our experiences as behaviorists have suggested in the past. Instead, we come equipped with predisposed tendencies imprinted in our neural pathways formed a long time ago through the lengthy evolution of human genes. These predispositions do not mean that environmental factors are not important—they are. However, as we soon discover, genetics plays a more significant role than some have previously speculated.

These prearranged bundles of brain circuits are referred to by several labels, including prepared learning, epigenetic rules, and innate drives. They are not the same as some of our hard-wired instincts but are more general algorithms. In other words, evolution has broadened human instincts, not completely eliminated them. For example, natural selection designed us to favor foods that are nutritious but that used to be scarce, such as salt, sugars, and fats. We crave these ingredients but are free to decide if and how much we should consume.

From a general perspective, innate drives have evolved and are activated or suppressed by a process called *circular causality*, a term used by Scott Kelso (1995) in *Dynamic Patterns*. Circular causality refers to the phenomenon when an organism affects its environment and, in turn, is influenced or altered by its surroundings. As this interchange continues over time, all players change as the circumstances dictate. Circular causality is the basis for self-organization among molecules, cells, organs, and social systems. Hence, it is one of the most fundamental principles used throughout this book in showing the vital links among human nature, voluntary cooperation, and intellectual capital.

Although he does not use the term circular causality, world-renowned sociobiologist Edward O. Wilson (1998) uses the same principle in explaining gene-culture co-evolution in demonstrating the development of epigenetic rules or innate drives in humans. He states that:

> In gene-culture co-evolution as now conceived by biologists and social scientists, causal events ripple out from the genes to the cells to tissues and thence to brain behavior. By interaction with the physical environment and pre-existing culture, they bias further evolution of the culture. But this sequence—composing what the genes do to culture by way of epigenesis—is only half the circle. The other half is what culture does to the genes. The question posed by the second half of the co-evolutionary circle is how culture helps to select the mutating and recombining genes that underlie human nature.

In defining gene-culture co-evolution, we must recall that no scientific evidence proves that *Homo sapiens* has anatomically changed in roughly the preceding 200 thousand years. Essentially, our species has remained biologically stable, but our cultures have been drastically altered by us in the past fifteen thousand years or so with the advent of agriculture and the domestication of animals, which subsequently led to the development of increasingly larger civilizations. Consequently, since evolution takes hundreds of thousands or millions of years to effect changes, our cultures have outstripped our innate drives in our recent history. No wonder we are experiencing such difficulties in living within the self-imposed constraints of our existing social institutions.

HUMAN NATURE

If we want to take advantage of the positive synergy of voluntary, collaborative behavior within organizations for the generation of intellectual wealth, we need to know three key aspects of human nature. First, we need to grasp the vital function of the genes. Second, we need to be aware of how our multilevel minds process information received through our senses. Finally, we should be familiar with some of our fundamental drives. Chapter 3 provides greater detail in these areas.

Fundamentally, all of our physical and behavioral characteristics are coded for in our genomes, which are all the deoxyribonucleic acid (DNA) contained within each cell of our bodies. By definition, each cell has one genome or a complete set of DNA distributed among 23 pairs of chromosomes (a set of threadlike structures). The DNA of each cell consists of three billion nucleic parts. However, only approximately 50 to 100 thousand of the DNA components are considered to be "working genes"; the rest seem to serve in a supporting role for the genes.

The deciphering and application of the genetic code is referred to as the *activation* or *expression* of genes. Genes are activated or suppressed in response to environmental signals, which can be electrical (in the central nervous system), chemical (intake of food), or tactile (touch). After receiving a signal, the information contained within the appropriate gene is copied. This process, called *transcription*, involves a specific molecule, ribonucleic acid (RNA), that acts as an exact copy of the gene involved.

Copying the DNA is required for expression so that the genetic information can be transported from the nucleus of the cell (the genome compartment) to another area of the cell (the cytoplasm), where it is deciphered into a functional product—a protein molecule. One key aspect of gene expression is that a single gene can be copied into hundreds of RNA molecules, which can then be translated into thousands of protein molecules. The level of amplification of the genetic information through expression correlates with the amount and duration of the environmental signal that is experienced. The process of deciphering and applying genetic codes is a vivid example of circular causality in action.

Humans have approximately 100 thousand varieties of protein, which are considered to be the essentials for life. According to Edward O. Wilson (1998), these proteins "give form to the body, hold it together by collagen sinews, move it by muscle, catalyze all its animating chemical reactions, transport oxygen to all its parts, arm the immune system, and carry signals by which the brain scans the environment and mediates behavior." Thus, everything we do physically or mentally alone or socially can only be accomplished by means of gene expression.

Further, a person's manifest characteristics or phenotype is not determined by individual genes alone, as suggested by classic Mendelian genetics; that is, one gene for every trait. Instead, phenotype is a complex interaction among all the genes (genotype), the amount and time of expression of the genes, and the environment in which the individual develops. In fact, the complexity is so enormous that, according to Philip Kitcher (1996), author of *The Lives to Come: The Genetic Revolution and Human Possibilities*, "virtually all the details of the processes through which phenotypes emerge are unknown."

Whether certain genes are activated or suppressed depends largely on the environment in which a cell or individual (as a mass of cells) finds itself. The circumstances in which one lives within the environment have both a psychological and a biological component.

Fundamentally, asking what is more important, nature or nurture, makes little sense. Wray Herbert (1997) of *U.S. News and World Report* makes this point very clear:

> The relative contributions of genes and the environment are not additive, as in such-and-such a percentage of nature, such-and-such a percentage of experience; that's the old view, no longer credited. Nor is it true that full genetic expression happens once, around birth, after which we take our genetic legacy into the world to see how far it gets us. Genes produce proteins throughout the lifespan, in many different environments, or they don't produce those proteins, depending on how rich or harsh or impoverished those environments are.

So, how does all this genetic information relate to voluntary collaboration and intellectual capital? Even after the human genome (the totality of our genetic framework) has been fully deciphered, the processes through which phenotypes emerge will still be unknown because of their enormous complexity. For example, roughly 100 trillion cells constitute the human organism, and individual cells continually interact with their immediate "neighbors." Trying to control such a system is illogical. Therefore, our primary focus should be on the organizational context and how it can support positive emergent behavior. As suggested by Kitcher (1996):

> An unknown array of causes probably sets up in each of us neural structures that determine our tolerance of environmental stress. Placid people, even when placed in desolate, threatening circumstances, will not be flooded with hormones that trigger eruptions of violence. Others, with lower thresholds, might well be able to live serenely in the supportive surroundings.

We also need to briefly examine the multilevel functioning of our brains. The human brain is the result of approximately 500 million years of constant trial and error. Scientists have traced this long and unbroken sequence back to the evolution of fish, progressing from those to amphibians, reptiles, primitive mammals, primates, hominids (our ancient ancestors), and finally to *Homo sapiens*. In the past two million years, the evolution of the brain has accelerated, eventually leading to its capacity for language and the development of multiple cultures by modern humans.

The full appreciation of the puzzle of the brain requires an understanding of the manner in which our minds function. This understanding is important from the perspective of how we respond cognitively to our surroundings, which involves perception, memory, and learning as we try to make sense of the world around us. As *Multimind* author Robert Ornstein (1986) makes clear, "consciousness is by necessity extremely limited and, therefore, only a small portion of the mind operates on the main stage at once. Thus, our minds are easily altered, our judgments shifted from moment to moment, by the way in which problems are framed and by which portion of the mind is operating at a given instant."

As suggested by MacLean (1973), our brain is structured in three layers. The lowest level, the brainstem, reached its current state approximately 400 to 500 million years ago. The brainstem is generally responsible for life support (such as breathing) and alertness. It also governs behavior such as domination, territoriality, threat displays, and mating. The second layer, the limbic system, resides on top of the brainstem and evolved to its present level roughly 200 million years ago. We share this layer with all other mammals. It regulates more complex actions that ensure our survival, such as hormone levels, body temperature, thirst, hunger, sexual desire, sleep, and play. The limbic system also plays a key role in memory storage as well as major emotions of fear, anger, love, and attachment.

The neocortex, or top layer, is the latest addition to the brain, which began to evolve approximately 18 million years ago, reaching its most rapid rate of development in the past 2 million years. In general, the neocortex is divided into two hemispheres—the intuitive right and the rational left—and is referred to as the *conscious mind*. It does not control the other two levels, but instead it helps them monitor and select the most appropriate responses in reacting to and anticipating environmental changes.

The significance of this information is that although we are the most creative and innovative species in the world, we still carry much of our evolutionary "baggage" with us. Based on this evolutionary premise, we are geared for quick reaction toward external threats (real or imaginary) and slow to respond to today's gradually emerging systemic problems such as global warming, which may take years or decades before most people heed such predicaments.

We can easily comprehend how the two lower levels of our mind respond to situations reactively and how they have a tendency to override conscious behavior. Ironically, the activities in the neocortex are also prone to shortcuts, and whatever enters consciousness is vastly overemphasized. That reaction does not mean we do not have a free will, but little doubt exists that "we are primed to respond to what's on at the moment and sometimes we overreact," as Ornstein (1986) suggests. The brain, similar to the rest of the body, is a self-organizing system where all the "players" interact with each other. The brain's function is not mechanical.

The importance of the environmental context in relation to our mental activities now begins to make sense. Designing supportive organizational structures to limit overreaction and misinterpretation so easily framed by our minds is critical. The context of a positive environment is another way to ensure that our affiliative drives are expressed more prominently than our more primitive impulses. We only need to recall the last time we misperceived a touchy situation and our inappropriate response based on the misunderstanding to relate to this concept.

In fact, evolutionary psychologists have determined that many of our innate drives can be grouped into two very general categories. For simplicity, I label them as the *self-centered* and *other-centered* sides. Which side is expressed more at any given moment primarily depends on the context in which a person finds him or herself and his or her individual interpretation of the situation. Both sets of drives are defined in detail in Chapter 3.

Essentially, prior to 10 million years ago, evolution favored those distant ancestors of ours who had developed the strongest innate drives for sexual and predatory aggressiveness. Unavoidably, we have inherited some of these genes and continue to use them today, depending on certain environmental conditions. Dorsey (1997) of *Fast Company* reports that evidence gathered by researchers and consultants Naylor and Crittenden strongly suggests that:

> Contemporary management, in practice, is almost totally dependent on the Red Box [self-centered side]; without it, along with the animal impulses of fear and greed that it inspires, external motivational techniques wouldn't work. Yet the Red Box is ultimately self-defeating: it pushes and pulls the worker in two opposing directions. You work out of fear, and simultaneously resist the urge to work, also out of fear, knowing the process always ends with shortfalls and criticism. Every success will still feel like a failure.

The good news, of course, is that we do not have to rely primarily on the self-centered drives. We have built these "gilded cages" for ourselves. We are slaves of our own making. Thus, we can change our organizations as we deem necessary.

An even more grim aspect to self-centeredness exists. According to some evolutionary psychologists, as summarized by Herbert (1997), "We are 'designed' by natural selection to conceal selfish motives from ourselves—indeed, to unconsciously build elaborate moral rationales for our selfish behavior." A vivid example of this rationalization is the recent application of "ethnic cleansing" in Kosovo. Little imagination is needed to apply this concept to a work situation, especially one where some people clearly benefit at the expense of others.

The other-centered side of our innate drives also evolved for reasons of survival and generated a genetic framework for drives such as compassion, empathy, and generosity. Such impulses, however, are not automatically energized when we interact with other people. They are mainly reserved for relatives, for the dynamic of kin selection (perpetuation of one's genes), and for individuals who in the near future may respond in kind (reciprocal altruism). According to biologist George Williams (1966), "An individual who maximizes his friendships and minimizes his antagonisms will have an evolutionary advantage, and selection should favor these characteristics that promote the optimization of personal relationships."

Clearly, research in human nature suggests that intense kinds of voluntary collaboration or social capital can only be spawned in collectives composed of relatives or friends and friendship groups. The development of such close relationships requires a supportive environment and a considerable amount of time. Obviously, the formality, distance, and contractualism inherent in hierarchical systems are a tremendous impediment to the formation and maintenance of social capital necessary for the creation of intellectual assets.

The two sides of human nature can be directly related to organizational power and politics. For example, negative or competitive power and politics characterized by the predominant pursuits of self-interest, the need to dominate others, and perceiving situations in win-lose terms are clearly governed by self-centered drives. Conversely, positive or collective power and politics can be directly related to other-centered, innate human drives. Here, power and politics can be classified as *noninterference mutualism*. Thus, these activities are marked by the simultaneous pursuit of self-interest and the interests of others, or pursuing activities in terms of reciprocal altruism.

Again, we can draw numerous examples of both types of power and politics from our work experiences. Where we must compete individually or in groups for controlled resources (e.g., programs, budgets, rewards), we usually resort to self-interest tactics and conceal those motives from ourselves and others. Where trust and a pursuit of mutually beneficial goals are present, altruism prevails. Alfie Kohn (1998) is convinced that "of all of the extrinsic inducements, the most destructive is where some reward or status is made artificially scarce, so your chances of getting a reward are undermined or eliminated if I get one."

The need for increased emphasis on a noncompetitive context for organizations highly dependent on intellectual capital now starts to make sense. An environment that supports the activation or expression of other-centered innate human drives should give greater sustainable competitive advantage to a company because its people will most likely demonstrate greater interdependence, reciprocity, and mutuality toward one another. These social capital features are not guarantees for the development of higher levels of intellectual assets, but playing almost exclusively to the self-centered side makes far less sense.

In summary, with all the possible interactions and genetic expressions that can take place during the continued development of an individual, we can easily see why each human is so unique. Uniqueness shows itself not only in physical characteristics but also in the personality or how the person may interact with his or her environment. As stipulated, genetic changes take millions of years to integrate into our genetic structures; however, environmental impact on gene expression is instantaneous. The area of focus for organizations, therefore, needs to be on its context because gene expression does not end with the maturity of an individual but is a continual process involved in learning and communicating throughout life.

THE IMPORTANCE OF ORGANIZATIONAL CONTEXT

Life in general, then, at both the individual and group levels centers primarily around the management of scarce resources for the sake of survival. Some would argue that this focus is true only for our biological needs and not for our psychological needs—I disagree. I believe that disassociating biological needs from psychological needs is impossible—they work together. The basis for all needs resides in the expression of our genetic makeup. How does one separate the mind from the body?

In essence, we are born as complete self-organizing systems. As a species, we have evolved to a level where we constantly seek greater complexity individually and in interplay with others. A person is more than a wage-earner. We desire novelty and pleasure. Our creative skills and our ability to entertain or be entertained are also part of our survival framework. These skills and desires make life enjoyable and meaningful, motivating us to pursue increasingly higher goals. We all need some level of motivation to survive. I doubt anyone would want to live without occasionally experiencing some pleasure in their daily lives. Kauffman (1995), author of *At Home in the Universe*, put it eloquently:

> We all make our living—frog, fern, bracken, bird, seafarer, or landed gentry. From the metabolic mutualisms of legume roots and nitrogen-fixing bacteria, by which each makes nutrients needed by the other, to the latest research partnership between drug giant and small biotech firm, we are all selling and trading our stuff to one another to get our daily bread.

Basically, power stems from the possession of or access to desired resources. Whatever the resources involved (e.g., land, capital, information, knowledge, and skills), they have the potential to create dependence of one individual or group on another. What must be understood is that the choices we make in how we organize and manage our resources are the major determinants as to which side of human nature is primarily expressed.

Asking people in organizations to be ethical, compassionate, and fully committed to organizational goals is not sufficient to elicit the desired results. Top performance simply does not emerge without a supportive organizational context. Other-centered drives are unleashed spontaneously in response to specific situational factors, not by persuasive slogans. That relationship is why, for example, compassion, empathy, and trust are so critical for highly cooperative behavior. Such factors cannot be manufactured but require a nurturing environment that allows them to emerge spontaneously.

Humans are not genetically programmed to organize their efforts in a specific way. We have a choice of options in response to our environment. As depicted in Figure 2.1, those options fall into two general categories. In one configuration, access to the accumulated resources of a group is controlled by one or a few select individuals. I have labeled this the *controlled access* context. The other option also entails the pooling of resources, but all group members share responsibility for managing the stores. I call this the *shared access* context. Clearly, each arrangement uses a different power base—competitive

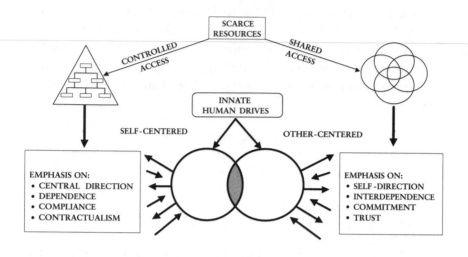

Figure 2.1   *Importance of Organizational Context*

versus collective—and, therefore, activates different combinations of innate human drives.

We must keep in mind that although infinite possibilities for organization schemes exist within each contextual category, the controlled and shared access modes cannot be mixed. The reasons for that incompatibility are simple. For instance, a hierarchy, no matter how flat, is still a hierarchy and belongs in the controlled access category. Conversely, any social collective held together by means of voluntary cooperation and without a formal structure, no matter how high or low its social capital, needs to be included on the shared access side. A closer look at the options in Chapter 4 further clarifies the vital differences of each option.

In Figure 2.1, arrows go in both directions from the innate human drives and back again from each contextual configuration. The arrows depict circular causality taking place between the innate drives and the specific organizational arrangement. For example, when an individual is immersed in a given environment, certain epigenetic rules are either activated or suppressed by that context. Suppose an individual perceives a work situation to be unsupportive or even threatening. This perception will mainly trigger an array of self-centered, innate drives causing that person to think and act selfishly (overtly or covertly). Based on that behavior, the members of that social setting will most likely also respond in self-centered ways, reinforcing the selfish conduct of that individual. If this circular causality continues for an extended period, that person's other-centered drives will have little chance of being expressed and strengthened. He or she may eventually believe that such behavior is appropriate for any work situation.

We need to recall that everything we do mentally or physically is carried out by the actions of our genes. That relationship is why change is so difficult to effect because it requires actual biological changes to take place within our bodies. Asking someone to "think out of the box" is easy. For a person to actually accomplish that goal is another matter. This example again illustrates why developing and maintaining a supportive organizational context is so crucial. Such an environment does not have to provide an exotic "fairy tale" setting; however, a strong sense of interconnectedness, altruism, and trust is required.

One more element of Figure 2.1 needs clarification: the area where the self-centered and other-centered drives necessarily overlap. The figure suggests that humans cannot exist normally without being able to express both categories of drives; therefore, social institutions should strive to support the activation of all the epigenetic rules in a balanced fashion. Undoubtedly, a greater chance of that balance taking place exists in a shared access environment because interdependence instead of dependence is its key component.

FOSTERING HUMAN NATURE

What are the key considerations in developing high levels of social capital or a shared access context? In response to that question, I have developed a general model. The basic model displayed in Figure 2.2 consists of four tenets for fostering human nature. The expanded version of this model is the focus of Chapter 5.

Essentially, the four tenets are fundamental competencies that an organization must develop in order to become capable of operating in a shared access or formal self-organizing mode, which takes time. The tenets cannot be "bought off the shelf." They must be nur-

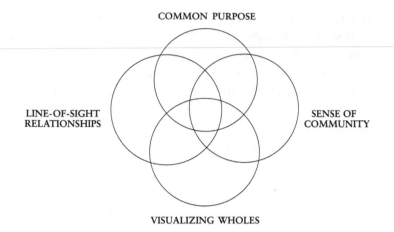

Figure 2.2 *Fostering Human Nature*

tured into existence because no step-by-step formula exists; every group consists of different people facing different situations. Artificially contrived methods and manipulation influence primarily the self-centered side of human nature and develop counterproductive informal networks. Self-organization, which voluntarily directs its efforts toward institutional goals, is only realized when the *other-centered drives* are also fully engaged. Basically, emergent behavior must be allowed to play out—it cannot be predicted or controlled.

As the model shows, the four tenets overlap and work in a continuously interactive mode, reinforcing each other. The system cannot function properly if one of the tenets is missing or has not been fully developed. For example, if no common purpose exists, then the system has no sense of direction. Without a shared identity, everyone will be marching to a different tune because no "chief" is present in a self-organizing system to issue commands. When people are unable to have line-of-sight relationships, they have little appreciation for important activities other than their own. Without face-to-face interactions, people have difficulty grasping the sentiments of other organizational members and freely sharing information. Again, we need to recall that the other-centered drives are only activated in the company of kin or friends; therefore, friendship groups need to have a chance to develop.

Visualizing wholes, and wholes within wholes, helps people see the big picture and appreciate the critical relationships among individuals and components of a system. Organizational members and teams are also better able to anticipate the effects on the entire network as they plan and implement changes in their activities. Consequently, without systems thinking, a self-organizing system becomes fragmented.

Finally, an organization lacking in compassion, a sense of interdependence, and trust has little hope for fully activating the other-centered human drives so critical for development of high levels of voluntary collaboration and the generation of intellectual assets. A supportive culture necessary for sustaining the personal feelings among group members also will not have a chance to develop. In essence, a community in which everyone feels a sense of true belonging will be lacking.

CONCLUSION

If business leaders are serious about developing high-performance organizations capable of prospering in the discontinuous environment of the Knowledge Age, then much closer attention must be paid to human nature. In particular, management needs to develop a more thorough understanding of organizational constructs that also support the activation of the other-centered innate human drives. Slogans and other enticements will not achieve this goal. These surface manipulations only intensify our reliance on the self-centered human impulses, competitive power, and negative politics. Counterproductive behavior can hardly be the desired result. A nurturing environment is a vital ingredient for the growth of intellectual capital, a healthy workplace, and for society as a whole because it caters more to the positive side of human nature. Ultimately, personal feelings do have a place in work and other organized activities. We should remember that other-centered feelings such as compassion, empathy, and generosity are not necessarily governed by moral rules. Instead, they are encouraged by the social context in which we live. The next chapter focuses on the brain and emergent behavior.

AN EXAMPLE

At the beginning of the 1980s, I was employed as an internal organization development consultant by a division of a large multinational corporation. The division where I worked was responsible for developing and producing two types of products: portable navigational equipment for the armed services and precision electromechanical controls for large commercial aircraft. Increasing production efficiencies and meeting tight schedules was of utmost importance to the organization.

In July 1981, I was given approval by the General Manager and his executive staff to implement a pilot Quality Circle (QC) program comprising six teams. Thus, I was off again on my white horse to make another hierarchical organization more human friendly and simultaneously more productive. I was assured by the General Manager that his "new management philosophy" placed greater stress on the participative approach, so I had little doubt that I would succeed not only with the pilot projects, but eventually with QC teams throughout the plant as well. I should have known better, especially after initially discovering that the organization, from corporate headquarters down, was more "rank" conscious than I had ever encountered in the military.

As I began the implementation process, the initial, and one of the most important, steps I took was to ensure that all levels of supervision were familiarized with the QC concept. This information was vital for two reasons: First, to be able to fully support or participate in the effort, all levels of management needed to know what Quality Circles were and what was involved; second, they had to become familiar with the concept to be able to answer questions asked by the people working for them. That goal was accomplished by 6 two-hour seminars. At approximately the same time, as the seminars were being conducted, all employees were informed of the forthcoming QC effort by a letter from the General Manager.

At the conclusion of each management awareness seminar, participants were asked to consider volunteering to form and become leaders of one of the six initial teams. They were also informed that the QC program would probably be expanded at the beginning of the following year to allow everyone who desired a chance to participate.

At the conclusion of all the seminars, I had amassed 15 volunteers willing to lead each of the 6 circles.

Final selections for leaders were made according to the degree that each candidate was motivated to experiment with QCs and where the individual worked within the division. Essentially, we wanted the pilot teams to be fairly uniformly distributed throughout the plant. Eventually, the six leaders selected represented manufacturing engineering, materials, finance, and three different areas of manufacturing.

Next, I met with each leader and his or her immediate work group. These sessions were conducted to familiarize prospective circle members with the QC concept and to ask them to organize teams within their respective work areas on a voluntary basis. Approximately 80 percent of each work unit volunteered to participate. I then conducted training for the circle leaders, which consisted of three full days of intensive off-site sessions covering leadership, motivation, group dynamics, and a variety of statistical and group problem-solving techniques.

Within two weeks following the off-site training, each newly trained leader had conducted his or her first training meeting, which I facilitated. This event officially marked the start of the QC program. The subsequent 10 to 15 weekly meetings were devoted primarily to training of team members in group dynamics, statistical techniques, and group problem-solving methods. Part of the time was also devoted to identifying work-related problems that would be prime candidates for the teams to solve once training was completed.

It was amazing how enthusiasm within the teams grew from week to week as they realized that they now had the autonomy to identify and develop solutions for problems. It was also heartening to watch people grow into *fully* involved and confident individuals, whereas before they had simply quietly carried out orders and instructions. Each team also tackled significant problems and devised extremely constructive solutions. But that soon changed.

I vividly recall one of the manufacturing teams identifying the excessive use of oil in their machining operation as a problem. That is, they thought a lot of money could be saved by recycling and filtering the oil several times before it lost its desired properties. The team quickly developed a solution to the problem and even identified a source where the proper equipment could be purchased. Basically, they determined that a portable sump-pump was available for roughly $7,000 that could recycle the oil in all the machines around the plant. The amount of oil saved would pay for the pump in less than three months.

The recommendation was immediately approved by the management steering committee overseeing the activities of the QC teams since the benefits were so obvious. However, because the idea did not originate from the Superintendent of Manufacturing, purchase of the equipment was delayed for months even after repeated queries by me and the Vice President of Manufacturing. I also soon discovered that the Superintendent, who had recently worked at General Motors, felt that the QC effort was absolutely useless and amounted to "coddling" workers. Eventually, the sump-pump arrived, but it then sat in a corner of the plant for another month or two before it was finally used.

That example was the initial "broadside" salvo to the QC program. Others followed, involving the other teams, essentially because of the same reasons. That is, management above the teams could not accept not being able to take full credit for the practical ideas emanating from the circles. Eventually, the QC teams withered on the vine similar to the job enrichment program I had been involved with years before. I can clearly recall the leader of the last team who was still determined to "hang in there" against all odds coming into my office and closing the door. He said, "Charlie, if I have any hope of being promoted, I have to leave the team since the Superintendent does not like the QC program even though he has never stated that out loud." Without hesitation, I replied, "Fold the team and get promoted." I knew the organizational context would not improve in the short term. It was time to call it quits and hope for a better opportunity in the future.

What happened? In a nutshell, the QC program, as a quasi-independent self-organizing effort, was designed to run parallel with the formal hierarchical system. From the start, management had no intention to change the formal top-down structure. Of course, we now know that hierarchies seldom fail to subsume formal self-organizing efforts, as was the case here. That is, hierarchies by their very nature will push such independent attempts at "unmanagement" underground because hierarchies rely mainly on position, reward, and coercive power for the attainment of organizational goals. Unfortunately, the resultant clandestine groups seldom support the goals of the firm. Are we doing better with the implementation of so-called self-managing teams and learning organizations? I have my doubts. It really is an all-or-nothing situation.

KEY CONSIDERATIONS

- Life in general at both the individual and collective levels centers primarily around the attainment and management of scarce resources needed for survival and the perpetuation of the species. That reality, however, does not mean we live in a "dog-eat-dog" world because chance and self-organization have a greater impact on biological systems such as us than natural selection. Fundamentally, reciprocity or circular causality reign, not mortal combat.
- Modern humans have not changed anatomically in approximately the past 200 thousand years, which means that our inherent genetically based predispositions also have not changed during the same period. That is, genetic changes take millions of years to integrate into our genetic structures, whereas the environmental impact on gene expression is instantaneous. Hence, the area of focus for organizations should be on its context since gene expression does not end with maturity of an individual but is a process involving learning and communicating throughout life.
- Only a small portion of our three-tiered brain affects our behavior at any given moment. As a result, our thoughts are easily reshaped and our judgments shifted from one instant to the next. Thus, we need to have work environments that limit overreactions and misinterpretations so easily framed by our minds.
- Most of today's organizational contexts cater primarily to our inherent self-centered drives. Therefore, we should strive to balance the self-centered drives with our other-centered predispositions in order for voluntary collaboration, which is so vital for the generation of intellectual capital, to take place. That goal

can be accomplished by adhering to the four tenets for fostering human nature.

- The options of how we organize our efforts to manage our scarce resources for survival fall into two broad but distinct categories: controlled access and shared access. We must understand the consequences of selecting either option if we desire to leverage intellectual capital for competitive advantage.
- Trying to control biological systems such as humans can produce unknown detrimental effects. For example, hierarchies by their inherent nature usually push overt self-organizing efforts "underground" because hierarchies rely mainly on position, reward, and coercive power for the attainment of organizational goals. These informal clandestine groups may or may not support the goals of the enterprise.

REFERENCES

Darwin, C. (1936) *The Origin of Species and the Descent of Man.* The Modern Library, New York, NY, p. 83.

Dorsey, D.E. (1997) "Escape from the Red Zone," *Fast Company,* April–May pp. 116–127.

Eldredge, N. and Gould, S.J. (1972) "Punctuated Equilibria: An Alternative to Phyletic Gradualism." In *Models of Paleobiology,* edited by T.J.M. Schopf, pp. 82–115. Freeman, Cooper and Co., San Francisco, CA.

Gould, S.J. (1996) *Full House.* Harmony Books, New York, NY, p. 214.

Gould, S.J. (1993) *Eight Little Piggies: Reflections in Natural History.* Norton, New York, NY, p. 304.

Herbert, W. (1997) "Politics of Biology," *U.S. News & World Report,* April 21, pp. 72–80.

Kauffman, S. (1995) *At Home in the Universe.* Oxford University Press, New York, NY, p. 15.

Kelso, J.A.S. (1995) *Dynamic Patterns: The Self-Organization of Brain and Behavior.* Bradford Books, MIT Press, Cambridge, MA, p. 9.

Kitcher, P. (1996) *The Lives to Come: The Genetic Revolution and Human Possibilities.* Simon & Schuster, New York, NY, pp. 240–241, 266.

Kohn, A. (1998) "How Incentives Undermine Performance," *The Journal for Quality and Participation,* March–April, pp. 7–13.

MacLean, P.D. (1973) *A Triune Concept of the Brain Behavior.* University of Toronto Press, Toronto, Canada, pp. 6–22.

Monastersky, R. (1998) "The Rise of Life on Earth," *National Geographic*, March, pp. 54–81.

Ornstein, R. (1986) *Multimind*. Houghton Mifflin, Boston, MA, pp. 12, 123.

Raup, D.M. (1991) *Extinction: Bad Genes or Bad Luck?* Norton, New York, NY, p. 185.

Williams, G. (1966) *Adaption and Natural Selection*. Princeton University Press, Princeton, NJ, p. 94.

Wilson, E.O. (1998) *Consilience: The Unity of Knowledge*. Knopf, New York, NY, pp. 91, 165.

3

Our Kaleidoscopic Mind

We cannot forever hide the truth about ourselves,
from ourselves.

John McCain

How do our 100 billion brain cells work together to create consciousness? We might also ask how do our genetically transmitted response strategies or innate drives function? How did these drives evolve and what exactly do they encompass? Knowing these biological answers allows us to develop organizations capable of generating high levels of both social and intellectual capital.

A NEW PERSPECTIVE

In describing the functioning of our brains, we must first admit that the brain is not the Chief Operating Officer in charge of the body for the same reason that a human being is not a machine that requires constant direction, monitoring, and control. The brain is simply that part of the central nervous system that resides in the skull. The brain does have a sense of purpose. Its neurons function for the same overall reason as all the other cells in the body. Essentially, the brain, similar to any organism, is an integrated collection of problem-solving elements organized to propagate their design through continuous self-organizing efforts. According to neuroscientist Scott Kelso (1995), "the system organizes itself, but there is no 'self,' no agent inside the system doing the organizing."

Self-organizing systems keep themselves on track by means of self-reference. From a social systems perspective, self-reference is a common vision *agreed upon* by all its members, or an "order parameter" in accordance with physicist and synergistics expert Hermann Haken's (1981) terminology. "The order parameter is created by the cooperation of the individual parts; conversely, the order parameter rules the behavior of the individual parts." In other words, "In an open system the individual constituents continually test new mutual positions and new kinetic or reaction processes, in which very large numbers of system components are involved." We are dealing with circular causality where the goal is noninterference mutualism. That is, self-organization involves a never-ending search for options that best support both the members as well as the system as a whole at any level of analysis.

Hence, environmental fluctuations (or chance) combined with the necessities of a given situation determine the *dynamic order* required for that event. Consequently, old relationships evolve into new ones and the fluid process cannot be governed by rules and procedures since the system and its members are constantly poised to seek new order in responding to changing conditions.

Again, in understanding the operation of the brain, we need to put machine-logic aside and begin to use bio-logic. According to Kelso (1995), "What we have here is one of the main conceptual differences between the circular causal underpinnings of pattern formation in nonequilibrium systems (biological and social systems) and the linear causality (mechanistic systems) that underlies most of modern physiology and psychology, with its inputs and outputs, stimuli and response." Thus, nonlinear arrangements work together simultaneously instead of in a sequential cause-and-effect mode.

Another way of comprehending this type of logic is that biological systems are parallel-operating wholes or networks. These networks consist of self-reliant autonomous members. As Kevin Kelly (1994) explains:

> "Autonomous" means that each member reacts individually according to internal rules and the state of its local environ-

ment. . . . These autonomous members are highly connected to each other, but not to a central hub. They thus form a peer network. Since there is no center of control, the management and heart of the system are said to be decentrally distributed within the system.

Circular causality is what gives a bio-system its tremendous flexibility and power. Kelso's (1995) research has shown that such a system "is poised on the brink of instability where it can switch flexibly and quickly. By living near criticality, the brain is able to anticipate the future, not simply react to the present." Another way of putting this concept is that self-organizing systems live at the edge of chaos.

BRAIN VERSUS MIND

Before discussing the relationships of the different levels of the brain, a point of contention needs to be set aside. This controversy deals with the age-old question, "Is the mind different from the brain?" The debate goes back at least two millennia to the ancient Greeks, but seventeenth-century philosopher and mathematician René Descartes has been credited with initiating the idea that although the mind depends on the brain, they are not identical. As neuroscientist Richard Restak (1984) suggests, "until the advent of PET scanners and evoked potential studies, it was possible to maintain the fiction that thought can occur independent of bodily processes. 'I think, therefore I am,' as the philosopher Descartes formulated in 1637." Ironically, the notion that the mind is separate from the brain is still largely accepted today.

This paradigm is experiencing a slow death for a good reason. How else could you explain the "mysterious" thoughts and emotions before the discovery of the electrochemical functioning of the brain? The currently accepted view is that brain behavior is the mind. The concept that the brain is the computer and the mind its program is definitely incorrect. Restak (1984) makes this point quite clear. According to him, the "mind, in essence, is all the things the brain does. To search for a 'mind' existing somewhere outside the brain is something like observing an Olympic swimmer and asking where in the athlete's body the 'swim' resides."

Further, the brain is not centralized nor does it have a center. That is, no seat of consciousness exists within the brain. For instance, "memories are like emergent events summed out of many discrete, unmemory-like fragments stored in the brain. These pieces of half-thoughts have no fixed homes; they abide throughout the brain." Kelly (1994) concludes that "our consciousness creates the present, just as it creates the past, from many distributed clues scattered in our minds." As we will see shortly, all cognitive processes are very tightly coupled to perception.

LEVELS OF THE BRAIN

Weighing in at three pounds and containing from ten to one hundred billion neurons, each connected to hundreds of thousands of other nerve cells, the brain is an unimaginably intricate web with a billion billion connections. Unquestionably, this network of electrical and chemical activities is the current information processing champion of the universe. In fact, it is a miniature universe, just like the individual cell.

With such tremendous power, the human brain has the capacity to store more knowledge than all the libraries around the globe. It has been responsible for inventing everything from agriculture to space exploration and for creating masterpieces such as *Othello* and the *Mona Lisa*. Yet, unexpectedly at times, it behaves more like an idiot acting on the most primitive impulses or not thinking at all. Of course, that behavior is not very strange when one realizes that we operate at the molecular level in much the same manner as a sea slug. Above all, as concluded by Nobel Laureate Gerald Edelman (1992), "The brain might be said to be in touch with itself more than with anything else." Perhaps that relationship is why the brain's activities are not very predictable.

Since this chapter is not intended for aspiring brain surgeons, I will use Paul MacLean's (1973) famous model of the Triune Brain to quickly show the different levels and functions of the brain as the foundation for discussing innate drives. As Figure 3.1 depicts, the human brain consists of three fundamental levels. In fact, MacLean suggests that we do not have only one brain, but rather three very

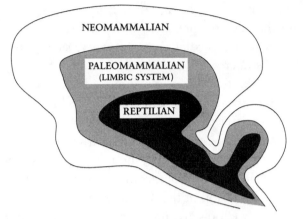

Figure 3.1 *MacLean's Three Brains. (From* A Triune Concept of the Brain Behavior *by Paul D. MacLean. Copyright © 1973 by University of Toronto Press. Reprinted by permission of University of Toronto Press.)*

tightly interconnected brains. Unfortunately, when reflecting on human tendencies, most people place primary emphasis on the activities of the cerebral cortex or the neomammalian brain, which evolved to its current state only within the past two million years. After all, who wants to admit to possessing a brain that takes us back to the age of reptiles approximately 500 million years ago? Or to a brain that evolved approximately 200 million years ago and that we share with all the other mammals? To admit such ideas would deny us our humanness.

So, we conveniently ignore the fact that at the level of the reptilian or hindbrain, behavioral responses are mostly governed by instinct and include regulation of breathing, heartbeat, and body movements. Here the focus is also on self-preservation and the preservation of kin, and brain behavior is in the form of domination, territoriality, threat displays, and mating. In evolutionary psychiatrist Bailey's (1987) words, the hindbrain is "where free will steps aside and persons act as they have to act, often despising themselves in the process for their hatreds, prejudices, compulsions, conformity, deceptiveness, and guile."

Moving up the ladder, we encounter the paleomammalian brain, or limbic system, that Edward O. Wilson (1998) calls "the master traffic-control complex that regulates emotional responses as well as the integration and transfer of sensory information." This part of our brain includes maintenance functions such as regulation of hormone levels, thirst, sexual desire, hunger, sleep, and play. The limbic system also performs a vital role in memory storage. "By this evolutionary stage, the major emotions of fear and anger have emerged as well as those of love and attachment." In addition, as evolutionary psychiatrists Stevens and Price (1996) further explain, "Conscious awareness is more in evidence at this stage and behavior is less rigidly determined by instinct, though these are still very apparent." The importance of environmental context in relation to the expression or nonexpression of the drives reviewed so far begins to become clearer. But we'll discuss more about this topic later.

The cerebral cortex, or neomammalian level of our brains, has given us our most human qualities. As Edelman (1992) explains, "The fundamental triad of higher brain functions is composed of perceptual categorization, memory, and learning. . . . Perceptual categorization is generally necessary for memory, which is, after all, about previous categorization." Learning, in turn, depends on categorization and memory, which also provides the capability to anticipate the future. In other words, the three functions are inseparable. The cerebral cortex is also involved with voluntary motor activity and the integration of other higher functions such as motivation and speech.

Compelling evidence exists that much of the neocortex in the past two million years has evolved in response to the need for increased *social complexity*, especially among primates including humans. The human brain, for instance, is roughly nine times larger in relation to body size than that of mammals in general. Our closest primate cousins, the chimpanzees, have a brain approximately six times larger than that of most mammals. What is even more pertinent, however, is that in most mammals the cerebral cortex accounts for approximately 35 percent of total brain volume, whereas in primates it varies from a low of 50 percent among some monkeys to approximately 75 to 80 percent in humans. Why?

Research in the past two decades by widely acclaimed psychology professor Robin Dunbar (1996) has revealed that mammals that maintain more complex social relationships have a larger neocortex than those that do not. More precisely, the quality instead of the number of relationships maintained seems to be the main determining factor of the size of the neocortex. For example, monkeys and apes are able to use complex patterns of social knowledge about each other, which they use to predict their behaviors in the future and then form relationships with others accordingly. These close social networks are established and maintained through mutual grooming. According to Dunbar, "only animals that have long-standing relationships groom each other regularly. It is an activity for friends, not for acquaintances." By spending approximately 20 percent of an average day grooming, higher primates (other than humans) are able to maintain highly interactive social groups up to approximately 50 to 55 members.

What about humans? Extensive studies by Dunbar (1996) and his colleagues have determined that the size of the neocortex limits complex collaborative social relationships by *Homo sapiens* to groups of no more than 150 people. Interestingly, that range was also the upper limit of the paleolithic hunter-gatherer clan size. If the only method available for maintaining relationships within these larger groups was grooming, then that activity would have consumed 40 percent of daily life, leaving little time for the other necessities. As Dunbar points out:

> Our ancestors must have faced a terrible dilemma: on the one hand there was the relentless ecological pressure [in Africa] to increase group size, while on the other time-budgeting placed severe upper limits on the size of groups they could maintain. It seems that somehow they managed to square the circle.
>
> The obvious way to extend the social circle, of course, is by using language. We do seem to use language in establishing and servicing our relationships.

Language allows us to talk to several people simultaneously. It permits us to exchange information, ideas, likes and dislikes, and other subtleties about ourselves. Language also allows us to talk about other people, permitting us to keep track of their behaviors without having to constantly observe them ourselves. "Language thus seems ideally suited in various ways to being a cheap and ultra-efficient form of grooming," contends Dunbar (1996). His studies further show that language seems to have evolved more to permit us to "gossip" in order to maintain a mutually beneficial social network and to achieve a balanced perspective on numerous conflicting interests instead of to primarily help us better coordinate our hunting and gathering strategies. As Dunbar concludes:

> . . . the human brain cannot sustain more than a certain number of relationships of a given strength at any one time. The figure of 150 seems to represent the maximum number of individuals with whom we can have a genuine social relationship that goes with knowing who they are and how they relate to us.

That is, humans have the capacity to assemble large mega corporations employing hundreds of thousands of people and cities with populations in the millions; however, as a species we are *physiologically incapable* of developing and maintaining mutually beneficial *voluntary* collaborative relationships within groups much larger than 150 people. In large organizations, relationships become fragmented, ties of common interest cannot be adequately sustained, and hierarchical structures begin to prevail. Consequently, from a human nature perspective, small size is absolutely essential for the advancement of social and intellectual capital in corporations. Our cerebral cortex gives us tremendous capability for social bonding, but that aptness is not limitless.

One more critical factor concerning close interpersonal relationships related to the physiology of the brain needs to be stressed. Humans come equipped with hormones that specifically promote trust and bonding—oxytocin and vasopressin. As psychologist Edward Hallowell (1999) explains:

> . . . these hormones are always present to some degree in all of us, but they rise when we feel empathy for another person— in particular when we are meeting with someone face-to-face. It has been shown that these bonding hormones are at suppressed levels when people are physically separate, which is one of the reasons that it is easier to deal harshly with someone via e-mail than in-person. Furthermore, scientists hypothesize that in-person contact stimulates two important neurotransmitters: dopamine, which enhances attention and pleasure, and serotonin, which reduces fear and worry.

Clearly, completely virtual organizations cannot be the answer for the Knowledge Age. They simply are unable to generate the necessary social capital required to develop the intellectual assets needed to stay competitive. In Chapter 5, I explain the vital importance of line-of-sight human contact as I hone in on the four tenets for fostering human nature and tacit knowledge.

Fundamentally, evolutionary adaptation has provided humans with highly developed mental circuitry for dealing with social problems. These mental models, such as vision, grammatical rules for learning language, and "mind reading" (the capacity to predict the mental states of others from their expressions, words, and actions), are part of our adapted brain. For example, compelling evidence suggests that the amygdala (one of the four basal ganglia in each cerebral hemisphere that is part of the limbic system) is associated with the evaluation of complex stimuli long before they are thoroughly scrutinized consciously (Allman and Brothers, 1994). This association means that we are born with specialized but integrated mental networks designed for solving problems encountered in our interactions with other people. However, the activations of these circuits are not precisely "programmed." Nevertheless, how the mental models are expressed or not expressed is determined more by an individual's environmental context than by his or her pure cognitive analysis of a given situation because we are roughly aware of only one millionth of the information that is processed by our brains. I will emphasize this point further in Chapter 5.

Several significant features about the brain need to be further emphasized. First, although the "three brains" are distinguished neuroanatomically and functionally, they are intricately connected; they work together, not independently. The "older" brains are vital to our existence and cannot be considered "excess baggage."

Second, a common misperception is that since the neocortex takes up 80 percent of the brain mass, it must be in control of the whole system. Not so. The neocortex began to evolve in mammals approximately 18 million years ago, reaching its most rapid rate of development in the past 2 million years. Its purpose was and is to help effect behavior that maximizes survival and facilitates the transfer of genes to the next generation.

Therefore, the cerebral cortex acts like a screen instead of a control mechanism because it is only one part of the self-organizing system. Because of its tremendous flexibility and capacity, the neocortex is able to make much better sense of environmental conditions, including anticipating the future, than the other two levels of the brain. Consequently, its power is in *helping* to monitor and select the most appropriate response by means of perceptual categorization, memory, and learning in response to changing environmental conditions. The neocortex cannot control everything because innumerable actions take place simultaneously. The eventuality of overall control would result in an immediate shutdown of the entire system and, hence, death.

Finally, the mind functions similar to a kaleidoscope that creates patterns, yet these patterns and our attention seldom stay focused for long. We do have free will, "but our conscious thoughts and actions are constantly modified by a barrage of signals from internal sources," as Restak (1984) suggests. As evolutionary psychologists Cosmides and Toomby point out, "What is special about the human mind is not that it gave up 'instinct' in order to become flexible, but that it proliferated 'instinct'—that is, content-specific problem-solving specialization—which allowed an expanding role for psychological mechanisms that are (relatively) more function-general."

OUR INNATE DRIVES

As concluded earlier, both human physical features as well as behavioral patterns are expressed in the genome. Carl Sagan (1977) said it best in explaining the relationship between environment and evolution:

> The development of human culture and the evolution of those physiological traits we consider characteristically human most likely proceeded—almost literally—hand in hand: the better our genetic predispositions for running, communicating, and manipulating, the more adaptive our tools and hunting strategies, the more likely it was that our characteristic genetic endowments would survive.

Sagan's ideas lead to a complementary consideration that innate human drives are not observable in terms of a single person. Rather, they can only be understood by observing interactions between individuals within larger populations. Essentially, one must look for universal traits as opposed to traits passed on from one generation to the next within a small family group.

In order to gain a better understanding of the innate drives, the following four questions need to be answered:

1. What are these innate drives?
2. In what type of a common environment did they evolve?
3. What are their general categories?
4. How are they expressed or repressed?

Innate human drives come under many labels. One of the most common terms is *archetypes*, but many other labels are used, such as innate releasing mechanisms, patterns of behavior, epigenetic rules, and genetically transmitted response strategies. These terms all signify that we all have certain predisposed and genetically determined behavior patterns in response to specific environmental conditions.

A distinction can also be made between ultimate and proximate causes. Basically, individuals come equipped with genetic predispositions (ultimate causes). However, how these predispositions are played out through life experiences (proximate causes) depends on the perceptions that a person has of the conditions in which he or she is immersed. That is, we are not born with a blank slate for a mind. Instead, we are born with an array of specialized neuron connections or adaptations in our central nervous system, which are subsequently reinforced or remain dormant as we interact with our environment.

For more than four million years since the appearance of the first hominids and for 98 percent of the existence of anatomically modern *Homo sapiens*, the dominating lifestyle on every continent was that of the hunter-gatherers. Human nature developed in this type of an environment. According to Margaret Power (1991), "Anthropologists consider the ancient foraging (gathering-hunting) way of life as the most successful and longitudinal adaptation humans have ever achieved."

To the hunter-gatherers, the best survival strategy under conditions of uncertainty, regional variability of resources, and high mobility was to function in small bands of 30 to 50 people. A tribe seldom consisted of more than 150 people. These bands were very tightly knit, extended, kinship and friendship groups loosely connected to an organic network in a general region composed of similar small bands. Because chance played a vital role in these societies, everyone lived by a strong ethic of sharing. The hunter-gatherers were extraordinarily egalitarian with no chiefs, hierarchies, or class differences. Their egalitarianism makes sense considering that during the last 10 million years, a new form of social interaction evolved among the higher primates and later in human groups. Instead of continuing to seek dominance by intimidation and the formation of social hierarchies, our ancestors began to use an altruistic strategy emphasizing affiliative behavior. As mentioned in Chapter 2, promoting the optimization of personal relationships gives an individual evolutionary advantage in passing on a greater number of genes. Therefore, altruistic behavior became a more effective long-term survival strategy than the use of threats and force.

In order to fully appreciate the altruistic side of human nature, we need to step back briefly to recall in more detail the time, place, and circumstance of human origins. Most experts agree that our lineage emerged in Africa, and from there our ancient hunter-gatherer forebearers eventually migrated to other places around the world. In the process, egalitarianism and the principle of generalized reciprocity or sharing continued to be practiced on every continent and in all kinds of environments.

Reciprocity was a vital social value of the immediate-consumption hunter-gatherers. In fact, anthropologist Lorna Marshall (1976) in her work with the African Bushmen observed that "the custom of sharing is so strongly established in the mind of the !Kung, and is so faithfully followed, that it has all but extinguished the concept of not sharing."

Food that was gathered was shared for several critical reasons. First, especially in warm climates, food had to be consumed within 48 hours of its collection. Second, daily hunting and gathering forays, which usually lasted for only a few hours, were conducted by small teams of three to four people who constituted barely a fraction of the able-bodied people of a band. The remaining members of the group stayed behind at a temporary campsite. Finally, because the foragers were extremely mobile, covering roughly 1,300 to 2,200 miles annually around a large home range, they needed to travel lightly without any excess goods.

One might assume that the immediate-consumption hunter-gatherers lived in totally communal social settings; however, that was not the case. A high degree of individual autonomy existed. Members of a group were fully accepted for what they were—skilled in certain areas and less able in others. Everyone was considered to be of equal intrinsic worth and capable of controlling and regulating his or her own life. However, individual autonomy was "balanced by a strong need for the company of others," according to Power (1991).

Individuals owned their own means of production similar to that of the knowledge workers of today who carry their means of production in their heads. That is, land and its resources were collectively used, but tools, weapons, and other personal items were the property of those who possessed them. Hence, each band member was an equal "partner" who assumed full responsibility for the success or failure of the group as well as his or her own actions.

No status differences existed between men and women. Although labor was relatively divided since men did most of the hunting and women primarily gathered, the division was pragmatic and not rigid. Hunting and gathering were ordinarily both cooperative events, and neither activity was perceived to be more important than the other. Therefore, women were equally independent, had their own areas of responsibility, and occupied positions of prestige just as well as men. Ironically, women today are still struggling to regain their equal rights.

Further, leadership was fluid and situational. Consequently, men as well as women assumed leadership roles depending on the circumstances. No chiefs existed to use their positions of power to enforce their will on others. For example, anthropologist Richard Lee (1979) once asked a member of the Kalahari !Kung if they had headmen. The man slyly responded, "Of course we have headmen! In fact, we are all headmen, each one of us is headman over himself."

The renowned anthropologist Marvin Harris (1989) in studying our past has concluded that "once we are clear about the roots of human nature, for example, we can refute, once and for all, the notion that it is a biological imperative for our kind to form hierarchical groups." Thus, in the hunter-gatherer societies, group activities and plans were made without any clear focus of authority or influence. These tribes, then, were truly fully "overt," self-organizing groups satisfying their survival needs through the process of circular causality.

Finally, analysis of skeletal remains and the observation of the few remaining foraging bands attest that the immediate-consumption foragers had more nutritious diets, were healthier, and lived longer than later herders and farmers. For instance, their diets were well balanced even by today's standards since only 10 to 25 percent of their daily food consisted of meat. The rest of the total calories came from nuts, fruits, and roots.

In addition, their lives were not as taxing as is stereotypically portrayed. As previously mentioned, only a few hours a day by a fraction of the members of the band were devoted to finding food. The rest of the day was spent resting, socializing, making music, and playing games. Approximately every six weeks or so, several bands would join for a festival that lasted several days. These large gatherings were periods of intense social interaction, including visiting, feasting, gift exchanging, and marriage brokering.

Basically, the "social capital" of the hunting-gathering societies was extremely high. As I have previously described (Ehin, 1993):

> . . . there was consensus on purpose and direction. Everyone had a sense of identity and connection. Interdependence, intimacy, equity, trust, and sharing flourished. The context of the day-to-day environment thus was one that promoted individual and team commitment. People were fully engaged, not only at the rational, but also at the ethical, spiritual, and emotional levels. Everyone assumed complete responsibility for themselves and the group.

Having reached its zenith approximately forty to fifteen thousand years ago, this "most successful and longitudinal" human adaptation—hunting-gathering societies—began to collapse. This collapse was brought about by the end of the last Ice Age beginning approximately 15 thousand years ago. Within roughly six thousand years, the great northern ice sheets receded dramatically, causing sea levels to rise to almost current heights. As a result, the flora and fauna around the world changed, forcing people to adjust to radically new ecologic conditions. Only the African Savannah retained most of its Ice Age animal diversity.

As many of the large mammals (e.g., mammoths, mastodons, steppe bisons) favored by the hunters for thousands of years gradually vanished, our ancestors had to make major adjustments in their diets. Consequently, they consumed a greater variety of small animals, more plant food, and seafood (e.g., fish, shellfish, and sea mammals). Also, with the flooding of the coastal plains and rapidly spreading forest landscapes, the hunter-gatherers were confined to increasingly smaller geographic areas and became less mobile. As summed up by anthropologist Brian Fagan (1990):

> As people adapted successfully to these worldwide changes, human populations grew. At the same time, the increasing complexity of obtaining adequate food supplies from a greater variety of plant and animal sources led to increasing complexity in human social organization. Both phenomena—population increase and greater social complexity—laid the foundations for the single most important human adaptation to the Holocene [postglacial times] world: the development of farming.

The advent of agriculture and the domestication of animals became the foundation for the proliferation of progressively larger "civilized" societies. What an irony: We gave up a successful egalitarian way of life in order to pursue our most basic reptilian instincts—power, rank, and territoriality—yet we call this movement "advanced" civilization.

Obviously, we come from a long social lineage and, therefore, crave close relationships and supportive settings. Reciprocity, or the "Golden Rule," has been etched in our minds with the rest of our other-centered drives for eons. Unsurprisingly, our paleolithic hunter-gatherer mindset has been on a collision course with the increasingly socially distant urbanized world of our recent making.

So, what are our fundamental innate drives and how are they categorized? As suggested in the previous chapter, two general categories of innate drives exist. Fundamentally, an ancient set of selfish drives dates back to the reptilian and mammalian eras, and another group of altruistic behavior patterns has been added relatively more recently.

As early as the mid-1960s, Bakan (1966) suggested that two contrasting "modalities" govern human socialization. He named these modalities "agency" and "communion," respectively. Later, Chance (1988), in his research with primate social groups, also determined two opposing modes of behavior work in social relations. He labeled these "agonic" and "hedonic." Most recently, Stevens and Price (1996) reached the same overall conclusion without labeling the two fundamental archetypes. Under the category of agency or agonic mode, Stevens and Price include "concern with rank, status, discipline, law and order, territory and possessions." Conversely, with the communion or hedonic ways of functioning, they list "concern with attachment, affiliation, care-giving, care-receiving, and altruism." I have simply categorized the two sets of mental architectures as *self-centered* and *other-centered*, respectively.

Other genetically transmitted response strategies exist, and many are yet to be identified. I would add several more drives to the archetypes proposed by Stevens and Price. Under the self-centered category, fear, anger, and sexual desire should be included. These drives are basic to individual survival. Remorse, shame, and guilt also belong in the other-centered category. These drives are universally apparent expressions that help to maintain an acceptable level of egalitarianism within a close community.

One more drive needs to be mentioned, but it is does not fit in either category or archetype. It is self-deception. Research in the past 15 years indicates that deception is an innate strategy for individuals acting on behalf of their genes. Evolutionary psychologists Nesse and Lloyd (1992) conclude that "the capacity for self-deception may offer a selective advantage by enhancing the ability to deceive others." How else could we justify gulags, concentration camps, ethnic cleansing, or taking deliberate advantage of people at work?

The final question we need to answer before we gain a full appreciation of our innate drives is "How are the drives expressed or not expressed?" The quick response is that they are basically expressed the same way as our genes, as explained in Chapter 2. The only difference is that here we are dealing with the functions of our brain, which is a collection of specialized neural pathways that perform different functions but in an integrated manner. The brain essentially is a jazz band composed of expert musicians who improvise around a common melody—survival—as they interact with their audience, or environment.

For a bit longer explanation, researchers are just beginning to make headway in gaining a better understanding of how innate drives are expressed, or for that matter, exactly how the brain functions. Therefore, in order to make an extremely complicated process comprehensible, I decided to use a theoretical model developed by neuroscientist Gerald Edelman (1992). Figure 3.2 outlines the conceptual framework of his widely accepted theory of neuronal group selection (TNGS). Basically, Edelman uses only three tenets in explaining his complex theory. "The three tenets of the TNGS [Figure 3.2] are concerned with how the anatomy of the brain is first set up during development, how patterns of responses are then selected from this anatomy during experience, and how reentry, a process of signaling between the resulting maps of the brain, gives rise to behaviorally important functions."

Before we take a closer look at the details of Edelman's model, we need to remember that the central focus of the higher brain functions is perceptual categorization, which is also tightly linked to memory and learning. *Perceptual categorization* allows people and other organisms to match their behavior to the demands of their immediate environment. For instance, we have the ability to quickly determine whether people approaching us are strangers or friends (even before we are able to see their faces) by the way they walk, dress, speak, and so on. The key point to remember is that recognition (perceptual categorization) is *selective* because, as Edelman suggests, "the world is not a piece of tape and the brain is not a computer." Perceptual categorization is not a mechanistic process, rather it is a serendipitous event.

But how then does "appropriate" behavior occur based on selective categorization? Appropriate behavior is the domain of our innate drives set by evolutionary selection. Essentially, our epigenetic rules are the internal criteria that "nudge" us (as opposed to direct us) to take certain kinds of action or to ignore or pay closer attention to

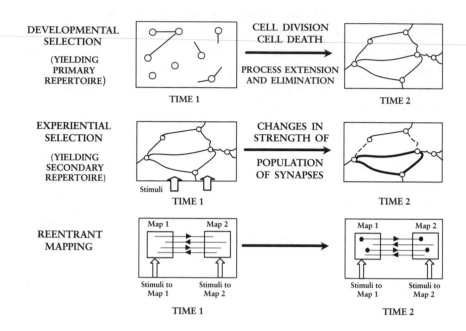

Figure 3.2 *Theory of Neural Group Selection. (From* Bright Air, Brilliant Fire *by Gerald M. Edelman. Copyright © 1992 by Basic Books, Inc. Reprinted by permission of Basic Books, a member of Perseus Books, L.L.C.)*

specific events as we selectively scan our environment. Deciding if a person is a potential friend or foe and whether to cooperate, resist, or ignore that individual is an example of our innate drives in action. Another consideration is that no two people read (categorize) the same situation exactly the same way and, therefore, their behavior also differs. Obviously, perceptual categorization cannot be controlled. If it could be, whose criteria (epigenetic rules) would we use?

So, how does perceptual categorization take place? In order to answer that question, we need to return to Figure 3.2. In following the three levels of the TNGS model, we must first observe how the fundamental groupings of nerve cells are formed during a person's development. At this stage of brain expansion, extraordinary anatomical diversity emerges as an individual matures. Even in identical twins, the neural networks that evolve are never identical because the process is so unpredictable and dynamic.

As Edelman asserts, "The genetic code does not provide a specific wiring diagram for this repertoire. Rather, it imposes a set of *constraints* on the selection process." We also need to remember that "even in a developed brain, 'sprouting' can occur, in which new neural processes form additional synapses." Again, we encounter circular causality, or self-organization, as cells divide and die, yielding our basic neural networks.

Next, the environment and experiences come into play. As depicted by the primary repertoire, the brain does not emerge as a clean slate—it comes equipped for action. However, which specific groupings of our neural networks are used more extensively than others is determined by our surroundings. For example, when information about the world is picked up by the senses, biochemical messages that link nerve cells flood the brain. In the process, neural connections are selectively strengthened or weakened in response to environmental signals. If, for instance, the same type of stimuli recurs, the chemical connections are further reinforced, allowing subsequent messages to be more rapidly recognized and categorized. Here we can begin to grasp how our innate drives are selectively strengthened or weakened by our environmental context.

The final part of the model is the most difficult aspect of the TNGS to visualize and understand. Here psychology is connected to physiology. This part of the model shows how through the process Edelman calls "reentry," or circular causality, the different brain areas "coordinate with each other to yield new functions." Thus, maps created during development and experience "are connected by massively parallel and reciprocal connections." As mentioned earlier, the brain is in touch more with itself than anything else. For instance, memories are not localized in a certain part of the brain. Instead, as Joannie M. Schrof (1997) of *U.S. News & World Report* suggests, "There are some local 'specialties': Different groups of nerve cells come alive to process irregular versus regular verbs, pictures of camels versus pictures of wrenches, an object's color versus an object's use. But a single memory or thought triggers many different parts of the brain simultaneously."

The *simultaneous* interaction among the brain's 100 billion neurons organized into specialized maps is where the power and flexibility of self-organization and perceptual categorization come into focus. No assigned "coordinator" oversees these maps. The motor and sensory actions are all accomplished by means of circular causality and the formation of order parameters among the circuits during the reentry process. The process is a classic case of "voluntary collaboration" because every player has the same common goal—survival and perpetuation of the species—and our innate drives provide the motivation to stay on track as we selectively categorize our environment.

To summarize, our complement of innate drives evolved to help humans cope with the context-specific situations encountered by our hunter-gatherer forebearers. As Stevens and Price (1996) stipulate:

> We know that behavior evolved first and that the capacity to make sense of it evolved later. We also recognize that behavior evolved to maximize survival and to facilitate the transmission of genes to the next generation . . . In other words, our evolved predispositions are committed to the perception of meaning, the selection of adaptive strategic options, and the consequential performance of socially appropriate or advantageous roles.

Thus, we come into this world not with brains that are blank slates but that already possess the fundamental bundles of neuron circuits capable of responding, at least in a limited way, to the demands of our immediate environment in a flexible self-organizing manner.

IMPLICATIONS

We must remember that our kind originated on the African Savannah and that we have not changed anatomically for more than 200 thousand years. Our innate drives evolved in a much different social environment from today. Egalitarianism, altruism, and trust were the primary ingredients for survival.

Only *relatively* recently have we drastically altered our environment and cultures. Unfortunately, the context that we have created for ourselves is diametrically opposed to that from which we evolved. Therefore, if we seriously want to increase the levels of voluntary collaboration in order to increase our intellectual assets, then we need to place much greater emphasis on developing social capital in our organizations. Fundamentally, we need to bring into balance both sides of human nature in order to accomplish that feat.

The importance of the environmental context should now be apparent. In an organization where rank, status, and possessions are emphasized, the most primitive innate drives are expressed based on perceptual categorization, no matter how much they are discouraged by official philosophy statements and other slogans. The model in business, unfortunately, has people fighting for their day-to-day survival because they are viewed simply as another category of expendables or employees. Continuation in this environment only reinforces expression of these primitive drives.

The opposite correlation is true in organizations where concern with attachment, affiliation, and altruism prevail. Here actions and behavior speak louder than words, and everyone is considered to be an important contributor or partner. In such an environment, voluntary collaboration and knowledge sharing prevail because higher order drives are constantly being nurtured.

I wholeheartedly agree with Carl Sagan's (1977) prediction that "the future belongs to those societies that, while not ignoring the reptilian and mammalian parts of our being, enable the characteristically human components of our nature to flourish . . ." Ironically, we have advanced science to the point where we are now exploring outer space. Simultaneously, we have been unable to develop large "civilizations" that have been able to withstand the test of time. Are we smart enough to bridge this large gap between science and human nature? In the next four chapters, I propose ways for bringing a brighter future to fruition.

AN EXAMPLE

I asked my long-time friend Carl J. Champagne, who is currently the President and CEO of Data Systems International, a small software developer and marketer, to provide two examples (one here and another in Chapter 7) from his rich and varied business career. Champagne is a seasoned executive with exceptional experience in managing large and small knowledge-based organizations. He was employed by GTE and for several years was the President of Digital

Equipment (now Compaq) in Canada. Out of frustration with the Industrial Age management philosophies of these large companies, he has spent the past 17 years as an entrepreneur guiding numerous small, closely held private companies successfully through critical phases of turnaround and fast-track growth. In the process, he has experimented with various concepts from participative management to teams and empowerment. Here he explains the importance of understanding the duality of human nature.

In the summer of 1991, I joined the board of directors of a 15-year-old privately held company that produced and marketed mission-critical financial and accounting software. It employed approximately 90 people, and its target market segment was small to medium-size companies. The organization was marginally successful at best; it had been floundering along since its inception. Its board consisted of close friends of the founder, including his personal attorney, family members, a supplier of personnel productivity services, and two senior employees. Of course, the founder was the chairman of the board; he had also chosen to manage the programming department. I was invited by the owner of the human resource management firm to join the board so that the company could benefit from my technical and business expertise in the software industry. I saw this invitation as an excellent opportunity to help turn a mediocre enterprise into a financial success for everyone involved.

After participating in the first two quarterly board meetings, I realized that the board functioned in an individualistic and self-serving fashion and primarily focused its attention on day-to-day operational matters. I had expected to see plans presented and acted on based on an overall business strategy. Instead, the agenda was peppered with functional issues and problems. The resulting discussions deteriorated into solving minute problems as opposed to providing corporate guidance and determining operational responsibility for the execution of agreed-upon goals and objectives.

With my personal aim of making a difference and achieving financial rewards from the opportunity, I set out to try to increase the board's effectiveness and subsequently that of the company. Fundamentally, I started from square one. We addressed the issue of a board charter—what this body should be accountable for and how its success should be measured. I also invited an outside facilitator to attend our meetings to help make them more productive.

These sessions brought interesting cultural and core value issues to the table. It became apparent that the directors were more concerned with their personal agendas than with the progress of the enterprise as a whole; consequently, little cohesiveness existed within the group. In terms of Professor Ehin's framework, the board members relied mostly on the self-centered innate human drives, and the activities of the group continuously reinforced the expression of these drives—a clear case of circular causality in action.

Part of the problem stemmed from the personal relationships these individuals had with the founder. Essentially, the founder's appointing of his close friends to serve on the board instead of selecting competent people from the industry or related fields resulted in self-serving and counterproductive behavior. As a result, honest opinions were withheld because members were more concerned with rank, status, possessions, and fear of offending someone. In this context, the other-centered innate human drives had little chance of being expressed. At the time, however, I categorized this behavior as political, deficient of character, lacking of individual values, and inability to participate in a team setting.

Consequently, I initiated team development and training for the board, which effected several positive behavioral changes. Interestingly, these sessions revealed the following basic issues and concerns of the directors:

I'm a friend. I don't want to rock the boat. The founder "knows" what has to occur.
The founder has never been there, done that, so what does he know?
I want as much as I can personally get out of this situation in the form of stock.
What does a lawyer know, I'm a doctor. What does a doctor know, I'm an attorney.

As a result of the team training, the board's effectiveness improved for awhile. What prompted the necessary change was a desire by the directors to be affiliated with the firm—to stay loyal to the founder rather than express concern for the welfare of the organization as a whole. Working with this company was definitely an eye-opening experience. I now grasp the importance of having the right people in place and of creating a supportive environment so that both sides of human nature have an opportunity to be activated. In Ehin's words, "recruiting people who are eager to develop and sustain a shared-access mode of operation."

I soon realized that the company could not reach its full potential without some major shifts in emphasis. Thus, I proposed a plan wherein I would assume leadership of the organization, which was accepted. Unfortunately, within two short months, the same problems as before began to resurface at the board level; we had slipped back into our old ways. The focus was again on operational as opposed to strategic issues. We were not exchanging pertinent information and ideas, and no sustained effort was made to move forward with innovative approaches in response to marketplace shifts. I now know I was faced with self-centered and self-reinforcing behavior.

I had to make drastic changes. To stop the hemorrhage, I clearly stated my expectations of the directors—stewardship, not control. My suggestions were ignored. I realized that I had to replace the board, and I did so within the next few months. Consequently, within approximately six months, I was able to make the appropriate changes throughout the rest of the organization. People were trained to form self-managing teams around core competencies, not functional areas. Those individuals unable to adjust to the self-organizing way of work with increased autonomy, but greater individual accountability, were helped to find other positions. New people were thoroughly screened to ensure that they were conscientious and willing to take on increased levels of responsibility in the pursuit of organizational goals.

As a result of these organizational changes, in seven months, annual revenues increased from a little over two million to five million dollars, gross margins from approximately 45 percent to almost 70 percent, and profits from a negative figure to 19 percent. We were definitely beginning to reach our potential. Thus, I had learned a valuable lesson.

Success in knowledge-intensive firms primarily depends on engaging skilled self-starters who are immersed in a supportive or shared-access work environment. Without "overt" self-organization, little knowledge can be generated to take a company to greater heights. Progress mandates a shift in "circular causality" from the self-centered side to more of the other-centered side of human nature.

KEY CONSIDERATIONS

- Humans are physiologically incapable of developing and maintaining mutually beneficial voluntary collaborative relationships within groups much larger than 150 people. In larger groups, relationships become fragmented, ties of common interest cannot be adequately sustained, and hierarchical structures begin to prevail. Consequently, from a human nature perspective, small size is absolutely essential for the generation of high levels of social and intellectual capital in organizations.

- Evolutionary adaptation has provided humans with highly developed mental circuitry for dealing with social problems. These mental models, such as vision, grammatical rules for learning language, and mind reading (the capacity to predict the mental states of others from their expressions, words, and actions), are part of our adapted brain. Thus, we come equipped with specialized but integrated mental networks designed for solving problems encountered in our interactions with other people. How these mental models are expressed or not expressed, however, is determined more by an individual's immediate environment than by his or her pure cognitive analysis of a given solution.

- Although the "three brains" are distinguished neuroanatomically and functionally, they are intricately connected; they work together, not independently. The "older" brains are vital to our existence and cannot be considered excess baggage. Hence, we need to develop organizational contexts that support the balanced expression of all levels of our brains.

- Perceptual categorization, which is also tightly linked to memory and learning, allows people to match their behavior to the demands of their immediate environment. Further, "appropriate" behavior is influenced by our innate drives, which are the internal criteria that "nudge" us to take certain kinds of action or to ignore or pay closer attention to specific events. Therefore, we need to understand how our innate drives are categorized and what generally is included in each category. That awareness allows us to conceptualize what factors need to be present to allow both the self-centered and the other-centered drives to be expressed in a balanced manner.

REFERENCES

Allman, J. and Brothers, L. (1994) "Faces, Fear and the Amygdala," *Nature*, December 15, pp. 613–614.

Bailey, K. (1987) *Human Paleopsychology: Applications to Aggression and Pathological Processes*. Lawrence Erlbaum, Hove and London, Hillsdale, NJ, p. 63.

Bakan, D. (1966) *The Duality of Human Existence*. Rand McNally, Chicago, IL, pp. 14–15.

Chance, M.R.A. (1988) "Introduction," in *Social Fabrics of the Mind*, edited by M.R.A. Chance. Lawrence Erlbaum, Hove and London, Hillsdale, NJ, p. 2.

Dunbar, R. (1996) *Grooming, Gossip, and the Evaluation of Language*. Harvard University Press, Cambridge, MA, pp. 55–79.

Edelman, G.M. (1992) *Bright Air, Brilliant Fire*. Basic Books, HarperCollins, New York, NY, pp. 81–94.

Ehin, C. (1993) "A High Performance Team Is Not a Multi-Part Machine," *Journal of Quality and Participation*, December, pp. 38–48.

Fagan, B.M. (1990) *The Journey from Eden*. Thames and Hudson, New York, NY, pp. 213–216.

Haken, H. (1981) *The Science of Structure: Synergetics*. Van Nostrand Reinhold, New York, NY, pp. 19, 236.

Hallowell, E.M. (1999) "The Human Moment at Work," *Harvard Business Review*, January–February, pp. 58–66.

Harris, M. (1989) "Life Without Chiefs," *New Age Journal*, November–December, pp. 42–45.

Kelly, K. (1994) *Out of Control: The Rise of Neo-biological Civilization*. William Patrick Books, Addison-Wesley, New York, NY, pp. 16–17, 22.

Kelso, J.A.S. (1995) *Dynamic Patterns: The Self-Organization of Brain and Behavior*. Bradford Books, MIT Press, Cambridge, MA, pp. 8–9, 26.

Lee, R.B. (1979) *The !Kung San: Men, Women and Work in a Foraging Society*. Cambridge University Press, London, England, p. 348.

MacLean, P.D. (1973) *A Triune Concept of the Brain Behavior*. University of Toronto Press, Toronto, Canada, pp. 6–22.

Marshall, L. (1976) *The !Kung of Nyae Nyae*. Harvard University Press, Cambridge, MA, p. 133.

Nesse, R.M. and Lloyd, A.T. (1992) "The Evolution of Psychodynamic Mechanisms," in *Keywords in Evolutionary Biology*. Harvard University Press, Cambridge, MA, pp. 601–626.

Power, M. (1991) *The Egalitarians—Human and Chimpanzee*. Cambridge University Press, New York, NY, pp. 37, 63.

Restak, R. (1984) *The Brain*. Bantam Books, New York, NY, pp. 144, 281, 347.

Sagan, C. (1977) *The Dragons of Eden*. Random House, New York, NY, pp. 98, 193.

Stevens, A. and Price, T. (1996) *Evolutionary Psychiatry: A New Beginning*. Routledge, New York, NY, pp. 16–17, 26, 49.

Toomby, J. and Cosmides, L. (1992) "The Psychological Foundations of Culture," in *Keywords in Evolutionary Biology*. Harvard University Press, Cambridge, MA, pp. 3–117.

Wilson, E.O. (1998) *Consilience: The Unity of Knowledge*. Knopf, New York, NY, p. 107.

4

Selecting Our Survival Strategies

Nothing ages so quickly as yesterday's vision of the future.

Richard Corliss in *Time*

In the last two chapters, I presented considerable evidence showing how human actions and behavior are grounded in the genetic makeup and innate drives of each individual and how their expression is in response to environmental conditions. I also pointed out earlier that people are not genetically predisposed to organize their social endeavors in a specific way. That is, we have a choice of options.

How an institution manages its vital resources, however, has a compelling impact on which innate drives become the primary basis for the behavior of its members. Therefore, the choices that we make have a direct correlation to the levels of intellectual capital, productivity, and satisfaction of any organized effort. As Nigel Nicholson (1997), Dean of Research of the London Business School, concluded:

> . . . having left behind our ancestral social systems, we have spent our [recent] history experimenting with new social structures which achieve imperfect compromises between our unchanging human nature and our changing environmental conditions. Much of what we study in social sciences—motivation, gender relations, stress, group behavior,

leadership, organizational design, and culture—can be understood and explained in terms of these twin forces.

Thus, we have been adept at developing all sorts of social frameworks for our survival since the Agricultural Revolution began, but so far we have rarely devised organizational constructs that also provide a good fit between the duality of innate human drives and these socially established realities. Basically, we keep forgetting that human beings come fully "equipped" to be autonomous, self-reliant, and able to pursue their goals independently and yet simultaneously have a strong need for the company of intimately known others. In order to prosper in the Knowledge Age, organizations need to cater to these two discrete qualities concurrently. So, in our recent past, what has been our record in choosing the most human-friendly and productive survival strategy?

SELF-INFLICTED PAIN

As one might correctly surmise, in the past ten thousand years, our ability to manage resources for the common good has been poor in comparison with the preceding 98 percent of our hunter-gatherer existence. Unsurprisingly, almost all of the well-known philosophers since the time of the ancient Greeks have written about the growth of alienation and the lack of freedom and creativity—two key human conditions—in our social organizations. Simply put, factors that facilitate human beings' realization of their essence have been almost totally neglected by our institutions. In other words, our other-centered drives have had little chance to be expressed outside the relationships involving our immediate family. A common example is the number of times we wish we were at home finding sanctuary in our families rather than at work. Literally, we have been slaves of our own making.

Let us briefly glance at recent history to get a sense of how dismal our performance has been. An appropriate start is to compare increased consumption with levels of satisfaction. Alan During (1993), a senior researcher at the Worldwatch Institute, reports that "people living in the 1990s are on the average four-and-a-half times richer than their great-grandparents were at the turn of the century, but they aren't four-and-a-half times happier." Why? Most of us have found that human happiness is not centered around more "stuff," but instead is primarily enhanced by factors such as "satisfaction with family life, especially marriage, followed by satisfaction with work, leisure to develop talents, and friendships." Essentially, these factors were important for survival in our ancestral past.

Further, the productivity of the U.S. workforce has more than doubled in the past 50 years. That is, we can achieve the standard of living experienced in 1948 in less than half the time. Theoretically, we would only have to work six months out of a year. Instead, we have chosen the opposite and strived to double our income, limit social relations, and decrease quality leisure time. "The consumer society, it seems, has impoverished people by raising their income," During concludes.

More than 17 years ago, Alvin Toffler (1982) drew similar conclusions when he showed that our industrial society has undermined an individual's need for community, a basic requirement of human beings. "As companies have grown larger and more impersonal and diversified into many disparate activities, employees have been left with little sense of shared mission. The feeling of community is absent. The very term 'corporate loyalty' has an archaic ring to it." In order to begin to restore a sense of community, Toffler suggested we must first recognize loneliness not as an individual problem but as a public problem.

Although some signs of change are encouraging, consumerism is still the driving force in our society at the expense of community. In our places of work, compliance—as opposed to commitment—is the primary means through which goals are pursued, and leaders use a carrot-and-stick style to get this compliance. Or, do this and get this, or don't do this and really get this.

Some would instantly respond by saying, "Yes, but organizations are getting increasingly flatter." That is true. However, what is the actual effect of a flattened hierarchy? Unfortunately, all we get is a little less of the same thing. Compliance instead of commitment still dominates.

For instance, an increasing number of people complain about how aggravating it is to call customer service centers where they are made to wait for extended periods, get little worthwhile information, and often receive a bad attitude from people answering the calls. Of course, this situation should not be surprising since these individuals work under extremely inflexible rules, which in many cases do not permit them to even go to the bathroom without permission from a supervisor. In addition, they must meet high quotas on the number of calls they answer, and they are well aware that, in many instances, they are working in dead-end jobs that are not valued either by customers or the company. How can anyone expect proper service and friendly attitudes from people who have to labor under those conditions? Of course, ideas for innovative products and services also seldom emerge in such organizational contexts.

Fundamentally, as Peter Block (1993) in *Stewardship: Choosing Service Over Self- Interest* states, "The ways we govern, manage, and lead are a testimony to self-interest." He further suggests that the actions needed to turn our organizations around are establishing a balance of power, committing to a larger community rather than self-centeredness, allowing each person to define purpose, and equitably distributing rewards. Essentially, we need to provide the proper social context where voluntary collaboration serves as the primary impetus for the generation of meaningful work and order without imposed controls, especially in knowledge-intensive organizations.

How can such a "soft" approach be more productive and profitable than the "hard-nosed" traditional way business is conducted? The response to this question is straightforward—because of our biology. Recall that among higher primates and later humans, new forms of social interaction evolved not to make us "saints" but to give us a more effective long-term survival capacity. In short, promoting personal relationships provides an individual with evolutionary advantage in passing on a greater number of genes. Therefore, our social institutions should take advantage of our innate drives instead of working against them by doing everything humanly possible to promote interdependence of their members through teamwork and even by designing buildings that "physically" enhance a sense of community. We'll discuss more about this concept in the next chapter.

I believe that the more basic question to answer is: Do we want to move ahead with evolutionary advancement, or are we serious about forcing ourselves to digress permanently into reptilian and mammalian modes by the way we structure our social institutions? In order to respond to this question meaningfully, we must first admit that modern humans are potentially both the most violent and compassionate beings on this planet. As paleopsychologist Kent Bailey (1987) connotes, although our "aggression is greatly influenced by socialization and culture, the primal causes of aggression lie deep within the recesses of the ancient reptilian and limbic brains. From these deep recesses emanate the primal motive forces which provide the impetus and energy for aggressive behavior."

One of the most gruesome recent examples of the aggression of which we are capable took place in Columbine High School in Littleton, Colorado. Albeit an extreme case, I do not believe our society wants to diverge farther in that direction. Therefore, "all factors, ideational and material, that limit the realization of [positive] human capabilities need to be examined and neutralized. The quest for empowering organizations must become part of all our social systems: political, cultural, social, and economic" (Ehin, 1995a). The smart way to proceed seems to be to "go with the evolutionary flow" by allowing more of our compassionate side to be expressed. After all, the most fundamental element of any organization is the individual; therefore, our primary focus needs to be on the positive side of human nature instead of on organizational machine efficiencies. We also need to remember that knowledge cannot be supervised or forced out of people. Without first establishing a solid social capital base, organizations have little hope of generating highly sustained levels of intellectual capital needed for survival in the twenty-first century.

OUR BASIC OPTIONS FOR SURVIVAL

Again, life processes at both the individual and group levels center around the attainment of scarce resources (including customers from a business perspective) needed for survival and the perpetuation of genes. I believe that only two basic methods are at our disposal in how we conduct the day-to-day operations of managing our vital resources. These strategies are diametrically opposed options for resource management. As stated previously, I have labeled the two modes as *controlled-access* and *shared-access*. Controlled-access refers to the centralized control of assets, including contact with customers or potential customers, by an individual or group of individuals. Conversely, shared-access involves the open exchange of assets by all members of an organization. This concept is all-important for the fundamental comprehension of what is discussed in the remainder of the book.

That is, the focus of any organized effort is the location, acquisition, and use of limited resources (tangible or intangible) for reasonable existence. However, in what manner individuals respond to such efforts depends on how the duality of human nature is expressed based on the conceptual categorization of a given situation by each person involved. Thus, any form of control will subconsciously impact more of our self-centered innate drives. Conversely, perceived autonomy to act in a specific circumstance will most likely bring about the expression of our other-centered innate drives. We must thoroughly understand that we can change organizational context almost at will but that we have no control over the expression or nonexpression of people's innate drives. Accordingly, trying to "artificially" impel individuals to cooperate voluntarily is illogical. This cooperation can take place only through self-organization.

The initial reaction of many people may be utter disbelief that only two options exist for resource management. One might immediately ask: What about choices between these opposite configurations? The crux of the problem is that the two contexts cannot be mixed. If we view an organization from a two-dimensional instead of a one-dimensional perspective, we see not a single continuum, but two. These two options are mutually exclusive because a person is either on a controlled-access or a shared-access continuum. People cannot be on both continuums simultaneously. Being able to accept and conceptualize the two-dimensional framework for organizational constructs is crucial for success in the Knowledge Age. The reason for this need is fundamental. "If we cannot visualize why we have to get off the 19th century hierarchy train and into the self-organizing information exchange, we will be unable to fully muster the commitment, constant learning, and intense interaction necessary for mutual growth and development" (Ehin, 1995a) so vital now and more so in the future.

For instance, whether tall or flat, a hierarchy—the model for controlled-access—is still a hierarchy that operates by means of centralized power and control over resources. On the other hand, a shared-access management entity functions in an overt self-organizing mode and is held on course by distributed power and a common identity. Managing via shared-access is best described by the well-known motto of the Three Musketeers: "All for one and one for all." Thus, as stipulated in Chapter 2, although limitless possibilities for organizational schemes exist within each contextual category, the two basic modes cannot be intermingled. When these modes are combined, the controlled-access mode usually dominates.

One more question needs to be answered before we closely examine how these basic survival options impact our innate drives and the pursuit of intellectual wherewithal. If the shared-access method of managing resources was so successful for such a long time, why did we decide to adopt the controlled-access context almost exclusively for our "modern" social institutions? Anthropologist John Yellen (1990) believes that the change was brought about mainly by the accumulation of excess resources—resources that exceeded the daily consumption needs and, therefore, minimized the importance of reciprocal altruism. The process began gradually and innocently.

As noted earlier, early hunter-gatherers consumed all edibles daily. At the end of the last Ice Age, as tribes were confined to smaller territories, they became less mobile and gradually began to till the soil and domesticate animals. This shift, of course, resulted in the accumulation of resources beyond the immediate daily requirements. Villages grew larger and relatively permanent. Consequently, hunter-gatherers were now faced with the problem of equitable redistribution of the stored excess to an ever-increasing population. The initial solution was to choose a trusted individual to perform the redistribution of the stores.

At first, the trustees not only worked harder than anyone else in carrying out their newly acquired duties, but they also gave more generously to others than what they kept for their own use (Harris 1989). Such activities persisted into the early part of this century as the "potlatches" of American natives of the northwest coast exemplify. Essentially, these trustees initially tried conscientiously to abide by the ethic of reciprocal altruism practiced for hundreds of prior millennia.

As societies grew larger and settled territories had to be defended from intruders, social stratification set in (Ehin, 1993). Eventually, the trustees became more powerful than the rest of the community members and retained increasingly greater amounts of accumulated wealth. With this retention came a more paternalistic attitude. Trustees could "take care" of others by fulfilling their needs and regulating their behavior. Kings, queens, and presidents emerged from this structure. Lastly, the entourage expanded to include CEOs and their executive staffs. The resulting controlled-access framework appears to have served us adequately during the agricultural and industrial eras but at a considerable social price. In the Knowledge Age, however, the controlled-access context has become less effective and even counterproductive.

THE OPTIONS AND INNATE DRIVES

Figure 4.1 outlines several vital considerations pertaining to the functioning of social organizations. First, it illustrates that only two primary modes exist for managing scarce resources needed for survival and the perpetuation of the genes. Again, they are the controlled-access and the shared-access modes. Second, the figure shows that the selection of either option has a direct impact on the structure that emerges.

In addition, the figure depicts how certain interactions and activities evolve within those structures founded on the expression or suppression of innate human drives. In fact, a circular causality exists between the environmental context and the drives, as indicated by the arrows going in both directions. That is, the modes activate certain drives that, in turn, reinforce the actions taking place within these processes. Finally, the figure clearly shows that innate drives overlap; thus humans cannot survive by using one category of drives exclusively. We exist best with both sets of innate drives being expressed. The issue becomes how to reinforce and promote expression of both sets in a balanced fashion. A closer look at each of these critical and fundamental considerations allows us to grasp the major differences between the two options.

Selecting the controlled-access mode invariably brings about social stratification. Why? Simply put, only a select few will be in charge of directing and controlling the management of scarce resources of

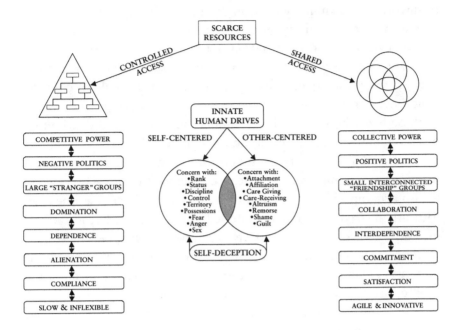

Figure 4.1 *Relating Human Nature to Organizational Context. (Reprinted with permission from* Business Horizons *[May–June 1998]. Copyright 1998 by Indiana University Kelley School of Business.)*

the entire organization. *Control* is the key word here. Therefore, no matter how humble the people in charge turn out to be, invariably they will be automatically perceived as the "ruling class." Such perceptions, then, will activate the self-centered drives of organization members. As a result, rank, territoriality, possessiveness, fear, and anger will dominate social relationships.

Controlled-access obviously produces an environment not conducive to family and friends or intellectual capital development. Here, social action, no matter how cordial on the surface, is based on competitive power, negative politics, compliance, and dependence at all levels of the organization. The controlled-access environment is permeated by self-interest and alienation. Although formal visions and philosophy statements may abound, the organization is usually slow and inflexible in responding to its environmental demands. This slowness is often due to a lack of common purpose. The signs promoting teamwork and commitment mean nothing in an organizational context such as this, and expression of these terms only promotes increased cynicism instead of mutual interdependence.

The lack of voluntary collaboration, responsiveness, and commitment by most organization members is not difficult to comprehend since considerable effort is expended on satisfying the demands of those few who control the accumulation, access, and distribution of all the key resources, including information. Naturally, vying for the restricted number of powerful positions (overtly or covertly) takes precedence over mutually beneficial cooperative effort. This process is also accomplished by small informal groups. Of course, these efforts are masked by innately grounded self-deception. For instance, I may help you complete your project on time, which appears altruistic on the surface, but I will make sure our supervisor sees that I took the initiative. Hence, the underlying forces are not based on altruism and trust but rather on competitive power and negative politics.

Obviously, in such a context, other-centered drives have little chance of being expressed. How can they when an individual is constantly surrounded by many relative strangers who mainly adhere to formal relationships that emphasize competition and self-interest instead of mutually beneficial goals as in friendships? Such relationships are similar to the daily aggravation most of us experience in trying to survive rush-hour traffic, where every driver is concerned primarily with his or her own welfare with little or no consideration given to other drivers. How can knowledge be expanded and applied in such an environment?

Selecting the shared-access mode of resource management, or "unmanagement," generates a diametrically opposite effect. For starters, social stratification and "class" differentiation are avoided. Rank and territoriality (but not one's status based on skill and experience) are meaningless in an organization consisting of partners equally responsible and accountable for the acquisition, accumulation, and distribution of resources. Noninterference mutualism is the name of the game in the shared-access mode.

The formation of covert informal networks with their potential for divergent or even counterproductive behavior is also bypassed because no difference exists between the formal and informal organization since self-organization is overtly practiced on a day-to-day basis. Further, the system is human friendly. It requires no expenditure of time and energy in climbing the social ladder, and little threat of direct competition from within exists.

As expected in such an environment, other-centered drives have ample opportunity to be expressed. However, the self-centered drives are also activated but less exclusively and in a much more subdued manner because all the activities of the social institution are directed at satisfying both individual and common needs concurrently. Undoubtedly, concern with attachment, affiliation, care giving, care receiving, and altruism become the underpinnings of organizational behavior. In addition, drives such as remorse, shame, and guilt also come into play, keeping members from focusing too much attention on self-centered activities and, in the process, limiting the need to use self-deception to rationalize behavior.

The resulting organizational context is opposite from the one formed by the controlled-access mode of managing resources. Collective power, positive politics, teamwork, and respect for personal autonomy instead of dependence take center stage. Everyone is personally committed to a common purpose, so the organization is agile and innovative in response to any environmental changes because goals and activities are commonly agreed upon. Within this atmosphere, the level of satisfaction usually is also high. In other words, the social capital in such organizations has the potential of reaching optimal levels, providing a firm foundation for the sustained generation of intellectual assets.

The organization can be large or small, as long as it is composed of small, autonomous groups of approximately 150 people or fewer who can be part of a tightly knit, more extended network in larger institutions. As discussed in Chapter 3, the latest scientific evidence strongly suggests that we have the maximum capacity to retain social "intelligence" of approximately 150 people, which was the upper limit of the hunter-gatherer clan size. Nicholson's (1997) research indicates that "in the average, short life [of a forager], an individual would rarely if ever encounter a stranger (i.e., someone from outside the kinship network of a clan). Our psychology is as a consequence geared to a known finite social universe." Therefore, "beyond the family, the number of people we cultivate as maintained networks are of clan dimension." Consequently, " a communications ethos is hard to maintain once organizations get much above clan size . . ."

We must recall that the other-centered, innate drives are only expressed in the company of kin and friends. "The result is a psychological orientation which is very much geared to defining group membership and who should be regarded as non-kin 'strangers.' The benefits of this instinct are the gratification of team work and the warmth of friendship with people we believe to be similar to ourselves (i.e., an "as if" extension of perceived relatedness). The disbenefit is discrimination against others we see as different from ourselves," as Nicholson further suggests. Also, as Robin Dunbar (1992) points out, "there is a well-established principle in sociology suggesting that social groupings larger than 150 to 200 become increasingly hierarchical in structure. Small social groups tend to lack structure of any kind, relying instead on personal contacts to oil the wheels of social intercourse." For instance, behaving unethically or not contributing in such small groups is almost impossible without being quickly detected and castigated by fellow organizational members. Therefore, placing limitations on group size is vital if we want to support voluntary collaboration and knowledge sharing. Such small intimate groups are ideally suited for maximum responsiveness in today's volatile, information-rich global environment.

Ultimately, the shared-access mode of organizational activity is the best means to close the gap between the needs of our unchanging human nature and the turbulent modern environmental conditions surrounding us. Moreover, the shared-access context is the most effective way of which I am aware to develop and maintain the close voluntary relationships required for high levels of intellectual capital generation.

In order to help you identify whether you work in a controlled-access or a shared-access environment, I have developed two boxes. Box 4.1 provides identifying features for a controlled-access mode, and Box 4.2 shows these same elements for the shared-access mode. Included in each box are approaches to maintaining order, work practices, and frequently heard comments. Besides serving as guides to identifying the two contexts of resource management, the boxes can also be used to categorize innate feelings that these modes generate.

BOX 4.1
IDENTIFYING THE CONTROLLED-ACCESS CONTEXT

Approaches to Maintaining Order

Most activities are expected to be predictable, controlled, and operating at optimum efficiency.

- Only a few key individuals have the responsibility and authority to maintain control by developing, clarifying, and reinforcing goals, action plans, and policies. Their task is to identify problems and prescribe solutions.
- Everyone is expected to diligently follow prescribed rules and behavioral guidelines in addition to embracing the solutions to the problems presented by management.
- All changes are made incrementally by the direction of upper management following rigorous formal planning and the establishment of precise implementation guidelines.
- Everyone is *asked* and *expected* to be a team player in addition to being dedicated to formally communicated cultural values.

Work Practices

People are given little autonomy in redesigning work processes that may be more challenging and rewarding.

- Education and training are primarily geared toward making current jobs more efficient and predictable.
- Little value is placed on developing and maintaining a sense of community that emphasizes intimacy, trust, and mutual support.
- Few people have line-of-sight relationships with other organizational groups and customers.
- Most people are not expected to understand the socially significant purpose and the overall interconnected operations of the business.
- Individuals and teams are seldom asked for input regarding how organizational activities, resources, and rewards should be managed.

Frequently Heard Comments

- You must.
- That's not my job.

BOX 4.1 *(continued)*

- You have no choice.
- Have you forgotten the deadline?
- We need to talk.
- It's the bottom line that counts.
- This is for your own good.
- Get off my back.
- I don't care how you feel.
- You had better pay attention to company policy.
- Don't you understand?
- Is it time to go home yet?

BOX 4.2
IDENTIFYING THE SHARED-ACCESS CONTEXT

Approaches to Maintaining Order

Chaotic synchronization is the basis for all activities; emphasis is on order through dynamic interconnectedness.

- Proper direction is attained and maintained through a collective mindset and self-reference (order parameter) and not by conformity or a "herd mentality." It is unity expressed through diversity.
- Everything is open to constant examination, experimentation, and improvement except the common purpose, which provides the necessary dynamic coherence for the community.
- Change is part of the everyday process. The organization is intended to operate on the edge of chaos, never in a stable, fixed point but continuously evolving in response to an unpredictable environment.
- Organizational members are considered to be *partners* responsible and accountable for all actions, including the maintenance of a common vision.

Work Practices

Mutual encouragement is given for constant examination and experimentation that may lead to more challenging and rewarding work processes.

- A strong belief that organizational strength stems from the synchronized effort of extraordinary people is evident. Consequently, everyone is expected to continuously attain new competencies that benefit not only the company but also the growth and worth of each individual member.
- Every opportunity is taken to strengthen the sense of community through mutually beneficial activities, interactions, and the sharing of sentiments.
- The pursuit of creativity and innovation is enhanced through the persistent encouragement of constructive dissent in an atmosphere of mutual trust.
- Systems thinking is pervasive. Interconnectedness of all proposed actions and continuing activities are diligently scrutinized to ensure effective common purpose. Everyone shares a part of the image.
- Every member routinely determines that all activities, resources, and rewards are equitably managed.

Frequently Heard Comments

- Can you think of other options?
- Am I on the right track?
- Let's take another look at that deadline.
- Thanks for taking the initiative.
- How often should we meet?
- We're in it together.
- What's your gut feeling on this?
- How can I help?
- Is this mutually beneficial?
- How does this support the overall vision?
- Please take a real critical look at my proposal.
- How time flies!

For example, by taking a brief look at Box 4.1, one immediately discovers that the key word describing this display is *control*. Hence, order is maintained (attempted to be maintained) by means of machine-logic or precision and predictability through centralized decision making, exact rules, and demand for compliance. Work practices provide little autonomy to people, training is primarily geared toward making current practices more efficient, and workers are not expected to have an integrated perspective of all business operations. In addition, frequently heard comments such as, "that's not my job" leave little doubt that the prevailing organizational context renders meager support for the emergence of large-scale, overt, voluntary collaborative interactions among company members. Consequently, the environment would provide insufficient social "nesting" for the generation of any appreciable levels of intellectual assets.

On the other hand, Box 4.2 is the antithesis of what is conveyed by Box 4.1. *Autonomy* as well as *interdependence* is clearly the fundamental principles for this construct. Bio-logic rules since order is maintained through self-organization or chaotic synchronization, common identity, and personal commitments. Work practices are governed by constant experimentation, a strong sense of community, and pervasive systems thinking. One of the frequently heard comments is, "we're in it together." Such an environment obviously provides the necessary social foundation required for the development of highly sustained levels of knowledge capital.

I am convinced that the maximum levels of creativity and innovation can be achieved only in an environment wherein other-centered drives are also nurtured and allowed to be expressed. This type of environment requires the neocortex to receive as much free range as possible by minimizing the need to activate our lower and more instinctive drives. Control by means of a high or flat hierarchy will not get us there.

NEW REALITIES

Before we decide which option to pursue, let us first summarize some important points. To begin with, living systems such as humans are endowed with the capacity to learn, to grow, and to self-organize.

Therefore, how this innate capacity is tapped is the key to the success of any organized effort in the future. More specifically, in a knowledge society, we might question which is the best course of action in accessing the highest sustainable levels of human intelligence.

Although we naturally self-organize in any environmental context, in a controlled-access mode our energy is sapped not only by our attempts to move up the infamous ladder, but also by the development of covert networks that we believe are necessary for our survival. We may have afforded such a "luxury" in the past, but in today's environment covert networks can lead to catastrophic results. As an example, stress in the form of absenteeism, reduced productivity, and compensation are costing American companies an estimated $300 billion annually, or roughly $7,500 per worker. How much further can we afford to take the controlled-access approach, both from societal and business standpoints?

I also want to emphasize again that the ever-increasing numbers of knowledge workers (approximately one-third of the workforce) are a completely different breed from the industrial workers of the past. They carry their means of production in their heads. When they leave, they take their means of production with them. Therefore, they need to be considered as partners instead of employees. How do you *force* them to "pick" their brains? How do you force creativity? These demands are impossible. Knowledge workers are *investors* in a company and not expendable means of production.

Finally, some people may suggest that strong leadership is the answer. As Hitler and Stalin exemplified, history may indicate otherwise. Recent management studies have reached the same conclusion. For instance, in one of the most intensive and in-depth studies of exceptional companies, James Collins and Jerry Porras (1994) categorically state that "a charismatic visionary leader is absolutely *not required* for a visionary company and, in fact, can be detrimental to a company's long-term prospects."

I believe that observation also applies to leadership concepts such as "stewardship" and "servant leadership." These concepts are useful for the transformation of existing organizations with the proviso that such leaders work themselves out of their assigned positions of power. If stewards or servants do not give up their hierarchical roles after completion of the turnaround, we are right back to where we started ten thousand years ago in assigning the job of resource management to a trusted individual. Must we constantly repeat history?

Leadership is an important part of self-organization; however, it cannot take the form of permanently assigned leadership. Instead, leadership should be situational and constantly changing, depending on what expertise and initiative is needed for the moment in response to environmental demands. True leadership cannot be founded on position power. Rather, it is based on influence and mutual benefit without the need to control the behavior of others.

In the end, as Wheatley and Keller-Rogers (1995) state, "The processes of life have nothing to do with machine efficiencies. They are fuzzy, redundant, and messy. Many solutions are sought in parallel. . . . But the messy processes and fuzzy logic lead to orderly solutions, because it is the nature of life to evolve toward more complex and effective systems." I see no better option than the shared-access mode of resource management in the Knowledge Age. Organizations that want to prosper in the future need to adapt the basic principles of this type of governance now.

At this point, I hope you understand that my proposal is not another grand scheme for a utopian state. First of all, self-organization cannot take place in a steady state. The process is dynamic and imperfect. The shared-access context does not eliminate mistakes, confrontations, missed opportunities, manipulative attempts by some individuals, or any other currently known organizational "diseases." All these side effects, however, can be minimized, and organizational social and intellectual capital-generation capacities can be taken to a higher level with the shared-access mode. In the final analysis, this option is much more practical and rewarding than what is in current vogue because it satisfies the human need for autonomy, creativity, and close social relationships. The following two chapters outline the key principles for putting the shared-access mode into operation.

AN EXAMPLE

I believe I am relatively well qualified to use our institutions of higher learning as examples of how to use (or not to use) the two general survival strategies presented in this chapter. After 23 years of service as an administrator in both the public and private sectors, I have spent almost 17 years working at Westminster College (an outstanding small private college in Salt Lake City, Utah), both as a dean and as a management professor. I also received my degrees from three different universities. Thus, I should be able to present a balanced perspective.

I would venture to guess that most of us view our colleges and universities as "bastions" of learning or where much of our intellectual capital is developed and disseminated. The record speaks for itself. They certainly have made a tremendous contribution to our society. However, our places of higher learning are also referred to as "ivory towers" or places of isolation and withdrawal from reality. That label also seems to hold true to a degree. What a disparity between definitions. So, what can we really learn about intellectual capital generation from these institutions? It depends. They seem to be an excellent example of the controlled-access mode of the Industrial Age. Consequently, we can learn a lot from their examples of why and how we need to change for the Knowledge Age.

Let me first qualify what I am about to say because I do not want you to misunderstand me. Essentially, 99 percent of the people with whom I have had the pleasure of associating within academia are the most dedicated and hard-working bunch of individuals I have ever encountered. After all, they have devoted at least three to five additional years beyond their master's degrees to further education, not counting their continuing research and studies to maintain currency in their chosen fields. They consistently go that "extra mile" to ensure that *their* students get the best possible education and counseling. They certainly are not in the field for the money. As one of my long-time colleagues repeatedly says, "I'm in this profession primarily for the psychic income that it provides me." All I can add is, amen!

Fundamentally, when we discover how to make our academic institutions more flexible and responsive to today's discontinuous environment, then we will be able to change any other organization no matter how firmly it is set in its ways. Basically, colleges and universities are faced with the same dilemma confronted by other established enterprises, but I believe to a greater degree. Must they forsake the traditional model of the industrial era and the enormous faculty and curriculum investments that have been made for decades, or can they get by with making adjustments to the existing systems and hope for the best?

In 1990, before stepping down as the Dean of the Gore School of Business at Westminster College, I assembled a forum of business school deans from the University of Utah, Utah State, and Weber State University in order to attempt to solve that dilemma and to develop a general framework for management education for the twenty-first century. Our response to the aforementioned dilemma was that "neither approach is appropriate for the long-run benefit of business education. Admittedly, a major paradigm change needs to take place, but not at the total expense of the current structure" (Ehin et al., 1990).

Personally, I was uncomfortable with the compromise solution to the problem. From numerous past experiences, I knew, although I wished otherwise, that the functional hierarchical system would prevail. I did, however, wholeheartedly agree with one of several recommendations on which we reached a consensus—to develop cross-functional modules that do not fit neatly into any specific academic discipline that would be team-taught to ensure that students receive a multiple perspective.

So, how far have we come in the past ten years? Not far enough, but that lack of progress is not only true of Westminster College. Most other schools are also still faced with that major dilemma, but the lack of progress is not due to lack of effort. Our current dean, for example, is an intelligent and energetic individual who is constantly looking for ways to improve the system. For instance, we have redesigned our core curriculum, consolidated and added majors, internationalized all courses, included information technology wherever possible, and so on.

Those cross-functional team-taught models that do not nicely fit into a specific discipline, such as accounting, finance, marketing, or information management, are still missing, however. Our faculty, similar to those in other institutions, have literally dedicated their lives to specific and narrow academic fields. Their survival or livelihood (based on their firm perceptual categorization) depends on their success in those fields and not on some interdisciplinary framework. That view is not only confined to the business school (although business is highly impacted by a rapidly changing environment) but also exists across the campus. For example, our Academic Vice President for years has attempted to prod the School of Arts and Sciences with assistance from the other schools to reform our liberal arts curriculum to make it more interdisciplinary and meaningful to all students who are required to partake in it. The results have been minimal.

The reason for this problem again is obvious. Why should the faculty in the department of sociology or biology or any other field give up some of its domain so that the curriculum can be integrated? How can they agree to something that will not or seems not to benefit them? Hence, we are back to the criticality of the organizational context. Until the context is changed to support and encourage cross-functional and interdisciplinary activities for the common good, not much can change without tremendous resistance. That context needs to include physically mixing the faculty offices among the different fields instead of housing the professors in their respective schools exclusively.

In other words, people need to feel that the best way to survive is to work together as much as possible. Therefore, our colleges and universities need to develop a common purpose that the faculty and staff can buy into that takes them beyond their individual disciplines. That common purpose can be achieved only through a shared-access context. The bastions as well as the ivory towers need to be dismantled. Our academic institutions, as well as other social enterprises, will have difficulty prospering in the new millennium without having the built-in flexibility to be extremely responsive to both their internal and external settings. In the next chapter, I provide four tenets that should make it easier for all of us to achieve that goal.

KEY CONSIDERATIONS

- The focus of organized effort is the location, acquisition, and use of limited resources (tangible or intangible) for reasonable existence or survival. However, in what manner organizational members respond to such efforts depends on how the duality of human nature is expressed based on their conceptual categorization of a given situation. Thus, any form of control (controlled-access) subconsciously impacts more of our self-centered innate drives. Conversely, perceived autonomy (shared-access) to act in a specific circumstance most likely brings about the expression of our other-centered drives. We must understand that we can change organizational contexts almost at will, but that we have no control over the expression or nonexpression of people's innate drives. Accordingly, trying to impel individuals to cooperate voluntarily through demands or slogans is illogical. This cooperation can take place only by means of self-organization. Therefore, only two general ways to organize our cooperative endeavors exist—using controlled-access or shared-access.

- In the controlled-access mode, social actions, no matter how cordial on the surface, are based on competitive power, negative politics, compliance, and dependence at all levels of an organization. This mode is permeated by self-interest and alienation. Although formal vision and philosophy statements usually abound, the organization is normally slow and inflexible in responding to external and internal demands. Signs promoting teamwork and commitment to common goals mean little in such a context other than promoting increased cynicism instead of mutual interdependence. Selecting the controlled-access mode also invariably brings about social stratification and the formation of covert informal networks with their potential for divergent or even counterproductive behavior. This contextual mode is not designed for intellectual capital generation.

- The shared-access organizational context, or unmanagement, is the diametrical opposite of the controlled-access mode of resource management. Collective power, positive politics (the above-board influence of other people or groups), real teamwork, and respect for personal autonomy, instead of dependence, take center stage. Everyone is personally committed to a common purpose, so the organization is more agile and innovative in responding to internal and external environmental changes. The level of satisfaction is usually high, and social stratification and the formation of covert informal networks are avoided. Rank and territoriality are meaningless in the shared-access context because it consists of partners who are equally responsible and accountable for the enterprise's success. In addition, no difference exists between the formal and informal organization because self-organization is overtly practiced on a day-to-day basis. Finally, drives such as remorse, shame, and guilt also come into play, keeping members from focusing too much attention on self-centered activities and, in the process, limiting the use of self-deception to rationalize behavior. This organizational framework is geared for the Knowledge Age.

- The shared-access context does not require strong central leadership. Leadership will never disappear from the organizational landscape; however, true leadership is situational and based on noninterference mutualism for the common good. Leaders have voluntary followers as they tackle a problem or an opportunity that also makes sense to others. Still, situations change and so should the leadership. Thus, every knowledge worker is a potential leader depending on the situation. Stewardship and servant leadership are useful leadership concepts for the transformation of existing organizations into the shared-access mode. Such leaders, however, must eventually work themselves out of their assigned positions of power and become equal partners in the self-organizing system.

REFERENCES

Bailey K. (1987) *Human Paleopsychology: Applications to Aggression and Pathological Processes.* Lawrence Erlbaum, Hove and London, Hillsdale, NJ, p. 384.

Block, P. (1993) *Stewardship: Choosing Service Over Self-Interest.* Berrett-Koehler, San Francisco, CA, p. xxi.

Collins, T.C. and Porras, T.I. (1994) *Built to Last: Successful Habits of Visionary Companies.* Harper Business, HarperCollins, New York, NY, p. 7.

Dunbar, R. (1996) *Grooming, Gossip, and the Evaluation of Language.* Harvard University Press, Cambridge, MA, p. 72.

During, A.T. (1993) "Are We Happy Yet: How the Pursuit of Happiness Is Failing," *The Futurist*, January–February, pp. 20–24.

Ehin, C. (1998) "Fostering Both Sides of Human Nature—The Foundation for Collaborative Relationships," *Business Horizons*, May–June, pp. 15–25.

Ehin, C. (1995a) "The Quest for Empowering Organizations: Some Lessons from Our Foraging Past," *Organization Science,* November–December, pp. 666–671.

Ehin, C. (1995b) "The Ultimate Advantage of Self-Organizing Systems," *Journal of Quality and Participation*, September, pp. 30–38.

Ehin, C. (1993) "A High Performance Team Is Not a Multi-Part Machine," *Journal of Quality and Participation*, December, pp. 38–48.

Ehin, C. et al. (1990) "The 21st Century Business Curriculum," *Utah Business*, June, pp. 50–54.

Harris, M. (1989) "Life Without Chiefs," *New Age Journal*, November–December, pp 42–45.

Nicholson, N. (1997) "Evolutionary Psychology: Toward a New View of Human Nature and Organizational Society," *Human Relations*, Vol. 50, No. 9, pp.1053–1078.

Toffler, A. (1982) *The Third Wave*. Bantam Books, New York, NY, p. 368.

Wheatley, M. and Keller-Rogers, M. (1995) "Breathing Life into Organizations," *The Journal for Quality and Participation*, July–August, pp. 6–10.

Yellen, J.E. (1990) "The Transformation of the Kalahari Kung," *Scientific American*, April, pp. 99–105.

5

Fostering Supportive Social Interactions

Remember one thing about democracy. We can have anything we want and at the same time, we always end up with exactly what we deserve.

Edward Albee

If going with the evolutionary flow as defined by shared access is the best strategy, especially in a knowledge society, then how do we get started on the higher level biological track? Or, from a corresponding viewpoint, if democracy is so desirable in our society, how can we begin to apply it more widely in the workplace?

We obviously need to acquire a much more balanced perspective on how human innate drives should be nurtured. Consequently, we cannot completely ignore our reptilian and mammalian self-centered drives, which are an important part of our brains' circuitry and are required for our day-to-day survival. Rather, the characteristically human other-centered drives should receive greater attention and a better chance of being expressed than they have in the recent past.

RETHINKING

The shift in emphasis from self-centered to other-centered drives can take place only if we completely *rethink* how social systems can and should function. This rethinking requires use of bio-logic rather than machine-logic in developing and maintaining our organizations. To accomplish this goal, we need to grasp the difference between order and control.

A tremendous difference exists between a typical machine and a biological system. Although still great, that difference is beginning to fade slightly with today's technology and "fuzzy" logic. Modern science, such as quantum mechanics and complexity theory, however, is not the basis for the machine metaphor that we continue to use as a template for present organizational forms. Ironically, seventeenth-century Newtonian "clockwork" mechanics still dominate our organizational thinking.

From a Newtonian viewpoint, a machine is constructed from well-defined and precisely assembled *interchangeable* components. These parts interact with each other in a predetermined way, specifying the function of the machine by its structure. Order, repair, and re-configuration is the responsibility of external control mechanisms or, in terms of social systems, management. Essentially, order equates to control and, therefore, a machine or organization is incapable of re-pairing, reconfiguring, or regenerating itself. The system depends on external direction and, according to design, is incapable of generating commitment from its components. Consequently, compliance *is* the mode of action of the components; if they do not work according to machine design, they are replaced. Clearly, this model is not very useful for today's companies to emulate if they want to be quick, flexible, and innovative.

Conversely, systems developed in accordance with bio-logic are considered to be parallel-operating and highly interconnected networks composed of self-reliant, autonomous members. Because the system's components are autonomous, they are not precisely configured or connected to each other in preestablished ways. They react individually, depending on the conditions of their immediate environment *and* on the demands of the system as a whole. The organization is in a constant nonequilibrium mode, poised for action and capable of repairing, reconfiguring, and reproducing itself. Without external control, order is maintained by means of an *order parameter* or shared identity (explained in more detail in Chapter 6), which is mutually defined by the distributed power of the network members.

Inherently, a bio-system does not depend on external control; order is perpetuated through voluntary cooperation based on a common purpose. This model is more sensible for current and future organizations where the intellectual content of every job is continuously increasing, and standardization constantly becomes less meaningful.

Rethinking, however, is not about finding new and better structures for organizing cooperative endeavors. It is also not about discovering a utopian way of social existence that is unattainable. Instead, it entails devising the most appropriate shared identity for survival in an increasingly volatile global environment. Robert Keidel (1994), an internal management consultant for Chevron, does an excellent job in summarizing the essence of such rethinking.

> The target of "re-cognition"' or rethinking is neither organizational units nor organizational processes. It is individual and collective mindsets, or ways of making sense of the world. Organizational cognition is conceptual, not numerical or technical, and it is a concern rarely pursued for immediate or even moderate-term ends. Rather, cognition is seen as the source of strategic advantage.

The key words in the above quote are "strategic advantage." The fundamental question becomes, then, what competencies can a company *leverage* to gain and maintain a sustainable competitive advantage? As previously mentioned, advantage does not necessarily come from advanced technologies, marketing, or production methods. These strategies can all be easily imitated, even in less developed countries.

What really counts is how an organization takes advantage of its "people power" by leveraging information and knowledge. The best way to do that is through bio-logic, or self-organizing systems. Shared-access systems, the closest parallel to self-organizing systems, are composed of members who are constantly positioned for action by continually testing new, mutually beneficial positions and reaction processes. Positive emergent social connections or voluntary collaborative activities that emerge from these systems provide true strategic advantage. Such relationships and the dynamic core competencies that are constantly created by such interactions are impossible for competitors to duplicate.

Organizations that have developed a shared identity are able to focus most of their energies toward developing practices that other companies find difficult to implement because their relationships are based on commitment, not compliance. Conversely, in firms where compliance prevails, information is infrequently shared, resulting in missed opportunities and preventing the growth of knowledge, especially tacit knowledge (discussed later in this chapter).

Fundamentally, only 20 percent of a company's effectiveness can be credited to proper strategy formulation. How that strategy is implemented, however, constitutes 80 percent of a firm's success. Therefore, failure to consider the impact of the organizational context on human innate drives is not only counterproductive, but it can also have a very detrimental long-term effect on the quality of work life.

Ultimately, organizations where other-centered drives are also cultivated have a much higher capability for "out-of-the-box thinking," or "strategic reframing." Matthew Kiernan (1993), Chairman of The Innovest Group International, clearly states that strategic reframing gives an organization "the ability to *transcend* competition altogether by completely redefining the rules of competitive engagement in such a way as to provide the reframer with at least a temporary monopoly over the critical success factors of the new game."

Basically, high levels of creative thinking that lead to new innovative products and services permit a company to avoid highly confrontational and potentially destructive head-to-head competition and instead help them engage in inherently more profitable indirect or niche competition. Interestingly, indirect competition was also practiced by the hunter-gatherers. No two groups, for instance, foraged in the same immediate vicinity (Ehin, 1995).

THE SOCIAL CAPITAL FOUNDATION

Based on my studies and experience, I have concluded that organizations must adhere to and apply four essential tenets in an integrated manner in order for a shared-access organizational context to evolve. The shared-access context, in turn, provides the solid social foundation or "nesting" indispensable for generating high levels of intellectual capital. These tenets are not a magic formula or a step-by-step process for organizational success, however. I have found no cure-all or quick-fix, even though many people are chasing such a phantom today. I advocate a long-term perspective to bring our social institutions more in line with our evolutionary underpinnings.

In other words, a shared-access context will not *eliminate* known organizational problems such as mistakes, confrontations, attempts at manipulation, or missed opportunities. Rather, I propose more meaningful ways to address root causes of organizational ills using bio-logic rather than machine-logic in identifying and solving human nature–related predicaments and consequently accommodate knowledge expansion. I am convinced that any organization (including government agencies, schools, etc.) that seriously considers the four tenets will be noticeably more creative and effective in staying ahead of the game in our global environment laden with uncertainty.

One additional note of caution is necessary. Following the four tenets is *not* for the faint of heart. Chameleons, martyrs, egotists, or people who are afraid of hard work will not succeed in the proposed environment. The shared-access context based on the four tenets gives comfort only to individuals who are extremely self-reliant and willing to commit themselves to demanding cooperative ventures.

Accordingly, enormous time and effort must be devoted to the selection process to ensure that potential members fit the organizational context. Fundamentally, people who are invited to join the organization need to be highly social, trusting, conscientious, emotionally stable, and open-minded. Further, they need to be willing to get their hands dirty, to meet new challenges head-on, to learn continuously, and to have fun in the process.

Now let us examine the four tenets that have the potential to amplify the strategic advantage of an organization by vastly expanding its capacity to leverage information and knowledge. As depicted in Figure 5.1, the tenets form a dynamic framework, giving the other-centered innate human drives an opportunity to be expressed but not at the expense of the self-centered drives. As a result, the system as a whole fosters more positive and intense cooperative behavior necessary for the development of knowledge assets.

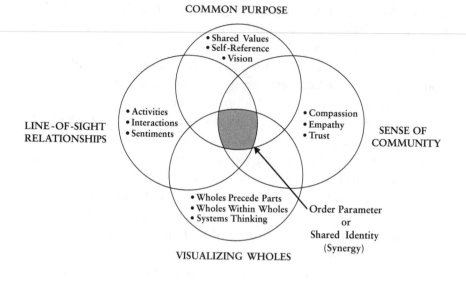

COMMON PURPOSE

- Shared Values
- Self-Reference
- Vision

LINE-OF-SIGHT
RELATIONSHIPS

- Activities
- Interactions
- Sentiments

- Compassion
- Empathy
- Trust

SENSE OF
COMMUNITY

- Wholes Precede Parts
- Wholes Within Wholes
- Systems Thinking

Order Parameter
or
Shared Identity
(Synergy)

VISUALIZING WHOLES

Figure 5.1 *Four Tenets for Fostering Human Nature. (Reprinted with permission from Business Horizons [May–June 1998]. Copyright 1998 by Indiana University Kelley School of Business.)*

Inherently, as suggested in Chapter 2, the tenets must be cultivated into existence because no step-by-step prescription is available, and every social arrangement consists of different people facing different situations. Also, as shown in Figure 5.1, the tenets overlap and work in a continuously interactive mode, reinforcing each other. Consequently, the system cannot function effectively if one of the tenets is either missing or has not been fully developed.

A further look at Figure 5.1 shows that the tenets located directly opposite from one another are more closely related to each other than to the other two components of the model. For instance, line-of-sight relationships pertain to individual members and teams of an organization who, in turn, are an integral part of a larger community. In the same way, visualizing wholes is almost meaningless without an understanding of the system's purpose. Again, all four tenets have a close dynamic relationship, but the opposites clearly complement one another more intensely than the other two. A closer look at each one of the tenets clarifies their vital interrelationships.

LINE-OF-SIGHT RELATIONSHIPS

The *most critical tenet* necessary for the expression of other-centered human drives is line-of-sight, or face-to-face, relationships. If you recall, other-centered drives are almost exclusively reserved for kin and close friends. The rare exception to the rule is exemplified by events such as devastating natural disasters when people compassionately but temporarily provide aid and comfort to total strangers. The opportunity to form closely knit friendship groups is extremely important, then, for nurturing altruistic and collaborative behavior.

Fifty years ago, George Homans (1950) developed a framework for organizational analysis that is still useful today. He suggested that the elements of a social system can be grouped into three classifications: *activities*, *interactions*, and *sentiments*. Activities are simply things that people do, or behavior that they exhibit, either alone or by interacting with other individuals or groups. Some activities may be preplanned or in accordance with certain laws and regulations, whereas others emerge serendipitously when we come into contact with other people.

Interactions are closely related to activities. Interactions occur when two or more people come together and have an effect on one another. That is, interactions take place when activities are linked together. Most often, but not always, interactions occur through acts of communication and can be differentiated by their duration, frequency, and direction.

Sentiments, which motivate behavior and shape perspectives about the self and the surrounding environment, cover a broad category of elements dealing with the internal state of an individual. Sentiments include values, beliefs, assumptions, and norms to which people adhere. We need to remember that sentiments are brought into a company by its members, and those sentiments, in turn, are molded by the context of that organization. The process is dynamic and two-way, or governed by circular causality.

Accordingly, line-of-sight relationships are indispensable for the development of two of the most fundamental factors that make the shared-access mode of operation so desirable—trust and the only effective means of exchanging tacit knowledge. As briefly discussed in Chapter 3, humans come equipped with hormones that are designed to promote trust and bonding. We also have neurotransmitters that specifically enhance attention and pleasure and others that reduce fear and worry. We are *physiologically* designed to be one of the most social creatures on this planet. Thus, an organization where people are unable to have periodic face-to-face contact soon becomes dysfunctional because its members cannot develop trusting relationships. Psychiatrist Edward Hallowell (1999), for instance, labeled these close encounters among individuals or teams as "the human moment." He stipulates that "the human moment has two prerequisites: people's physical presence and their emotional and intellectual attention."

According to Hallowell, "the human moment is like light in an otherwise dark room: it illuminates dark corners and dispels suspicions and fears. Without it, toxic worry grows." From a more fundamental perspective, "the human moment . . . is a regulator: when you take it away, people's primitive instincts can get the better of them." Again, we can see why completely virtual organizations cannot be the answer for future organizational success. Without trust and compassion, how does a company gain competitive advantage?

One more important aspect concerning face-to-face relationships must be emphasized: our epigenetic ability to interpret emotions from others' expressions. Our adeptness for "reading minds" is a highly developed capacity we all possess (to one degree or another) for selectively categorizing the intentions, emotions, presumed deceptions, and possible threats of others. As Nicholson (1997) stipulates, mind reading "has great functionality for regulating the complex social relations of human collective living. The greater one's skill in reading what others are thinking and feeling, the more able one is to forge bonds of trust, do deals, and avoid social threats." A good current example of our ability to interpret expressions is the job selection process, where impressions of a potential candidate are usually formed within the first few minutes of an interview.

The importance of categorizing line-of-sight relationships into the three elements prescribed by Homans, then, is straightforward. Without line-of-sight or face-to-face activities and interactions with members of one's organization, customers, and suppliers, significant positive empathetic sentiments cannot emerge.

The absence of mutually supportive sentiments does not give the other-centered drives a chance to be activated, and members of an organization are left in a context where the self-centered drives are primarily expressed. Therefore, no matter how diligently people are asked to perform in unselfish and ethical ways, high levels of altruistic behavior simply do not occur. In other words, when a company becomes too large to facilitate face-to-face relationships, it loses most of its capability for supporting the expression of other-centered drives.

Now let us examine the other critical factor in the need of line-of-sight relationships—tacit knowledge. We need to understand that intellectual growth and intellectual capital generation entail two types of knowledge, one of which most organizations have unfortunately overlooked up to now. Basically, knowledge is classified into two categories: explicit and tacit. *Explicit knowledge* is usually gained through sources such as formal education, training, books, and the Internet and has been codified or formally defined. *Tacit knowledge*, instead, is acquired by first-hand experiences or by working with more experienced people and is unrelated or unexpressed knowledge. Hence, tacit knowledge encompasses ideas and abstractions at the individual level. In my opinion, this abstract individual relationship has prevented our social institutions from giving tacit knowledge its due attention.

Without tacit knowledge, new explicit knowledge cannot be gained. Michael Polanyi (1958) is credited with developing the theory of tacit knowledge more than 50 years ago. Unfortunately, his theory was directed primarily toward the scientific community and, therefore, has received little public attention until recently. Fundamentally, Polanyi considers knowledge to be both individually and collectively formed in a continuous action-oriented process. That is, constant circular causality exists between personal tacit knowledge and explicit public knowledge as we focus our attention from one circumstance to another. Thus, he stipulates that "the adaptation of our conceptions and of the corresponding use of language to new things that we identify as new variants of known kinds of things is achieved subsidiarily, while our attention is focused on making sense of a situation in front of us." Polanyi also states that new discoveries cannot be achieved by following strict formalized procedures. For example, "the irreversible character of discovery suggests that no solution of a problem can be accredited as a discovery if it is achieved by a procedure following finite rules."

Several other aspects about tacit knowledge need to be summarized in order to emphasize the importance of line-of-site relationships to intellectual asset formation. First, expertise cannot be transferred from one person to another because each individual gradually builds up his or her own expertise in various areas over time. For instance, no one can teach another person how to ride a bicycle without that person actually trying to ride a bicycle him or herself. As knowledge management expert Karl Erik Sveiby (1997) suggests, "integration of knowledge is a personal skill. It cannot be disposed of or transferred; each person must build it up individually." He also postulates that personal knowledge provides an individual the "capacity to act." Hence, "the more skilled we become the more we can modify our rules of procedure," and eventually we can even invent new rules. That process is a good example of how "out-of-the-box thinking" occurs.

Further, "you cannot define and manage intellectual assets unless you know what you are trying to do with them," as stated by Thomas Stewart (1997) of *Fortune* magazine. Therefore, *common purpose* and *visualizing wholes* or systems thinking, two other of the four basic tenets, are important to generating intellectual capital. That is, you need to focus on a specific goal before related tacit knowledge can emerge in support of attaining that goal. Of course, tacit knowledge also has its pros and cons, so it needs to be handled with care. As Stewart points out, "the great virtue of tacit knowledge is that it is automatic, requiring little or no time or thought . . . But every virtue has a set of reciprocal vices, and tacit knowledge has three: It can be wrong; it's hard to change; and it's difficult to communicate." I must add that all three "vices" can best be kept in check by a well-functioning shared-access or self-organizing system and, least of all, by a hierarchy. Tacit knowledge is not useful unless it is made explicit and applied effectively.

In summary, tacit knowledge is an understanding gained by people through selective categorization as they continuously try to evaluate their surrounding environment. Tacit knowledge is part of our mindset or world view, which, once established, changes slowly over time. This knowledge is hard to convey to others, but it is also the foundation of new knowledge. Hence, as people apply their skills in pursuit of new innovations by interacting with other experts, tacit knowledge percolates and combines with the ideas of others to form new explicit knowledge that can then be practically applied.

Therefore, close line-of-sight relationships based on interdependence, mutuality, and reciprocity, which have a direct impact on our other-centered drives, are the key to the "gold mine" of intellectual assets. That is, tacit knowledge must be allowed to *emerge* through self-organization. It cannot be forced out of people because even they may not know exactly what they possess. Also, explicit knowledge can be copied, but tacit knowledge or knowing cannot. Consequently, developing organizational contexts that best facilitate the voluntary "mining" of rich tacit knowledge provides such institutions the ultimate competitive advantage. This knowledge is the only source for highly sustained levels of intellectual capital.

Line-of-sight relationships can best be accomplished by means of "real" teams. Such teams have *voluntary membership*, are well trained (both technically and in group dynamics), and are free to manage themselves. Real teams have a powerful positive effect on promoting individual psychological empowerment, which, according to Professor Gretchen Spreitzer (1996), consists of meaning, competence, self-determination, and impact.

"Meaning is the value of a work goal or purpose, judged in relation to an individual's own ideals or standards . . . Competency, or self-efficacy, is an individual's belief in his or her capability to perform activities with skill." Self-determination "is an individual's sense of having choice in initiating and regulating action." Finally, "impact is the degree to which an individual can influence strategic, administrative, or operating outcomes at work." A person needs to have a positive outlook in all four areas in order to possess an active rather than a passive orientation toward work; that is, "an orientation in which an individual wishes and feels able to shape his or her work role and context." Recall from Chapter 3 that we evaluate the world around us through selective categorization or perception. Therefore, psychological empowerment or a positive outlook in a social setting is an important factor in activating our other-centered drives.

Further, only close face-to-face relationships and teams allow organizational members to fully utilize the mutually beneficial growth that occurs when people interact. As a result, the net supply of social and intellectual capital is continuously expanded. Social science researcher Joyce Fletcher (1996) suggests that such intellectual growth requires three interrelated qualities: interdependence, mutuality, and reciprocity. First, "growth fostering interactions are characterized by a belief that interdependence rather than autonomy is the ideal state in which to achieve, grow, and develop . . . Implicit in this belief in interdependence is an acceptance of the responsibility to contribute to the development of others and a recognition of the opportunity to grow through these enabling interactions."

Second, "relational growth depends on both parties approaching the interaction expecting to grow and benefit from it . . . Achieving mutuality in relational interactions, then, depends on both parties having two sets of skills—skills in enabling others (ability to assume the expert role in guiding, teaching, explaining) and skills in being enabled (ability to step away from the expert role in order to be influenced by and learn from others)."

Finally, "reciprocity refers to the expectation that both parties will have the skills to achieve this two-directional model of growth and will be motivated to use them. That is, it assumes that both parties feel a responsibility and desire to be both teacher and learner." Interestingly, world-renowned author and lecturer Stephen Covey (1989) reached the same conclusion. He suggests that "as we become independent—proactive, centered in correct principles, value driven and able to organize and execute around the priorities in our life with integrity—we then can choose to become interdependent—capable of building rich, enduring, highly productive relationships with other people." Again, we encounter the hunter-gatherer ethic of sharing and circular causality of self-organizing systems in action.

SENSE OF COMMUNITY

Fundamentally, a community is a social entity that serves multiple needs of its members individually and as a whole. Its underpinnings are firmly lodged in effective line-of-sight relationships. Thus, a community is a safe haven or home base for a group of people with shared interests, where compassion, empathy, and trust pervade. It is a place where people know they are among friends and where individual values can be openly expressed. It is a place that puts a premium on enabling people to feel that they are making a meaningful contribution alone or as a team member. It serves as a "melting pot" for the generation of new perspectives, where criticism is encouraged but in an atmosphere of caring. It is a place where people truly feel that they belong and where our other-centered drives have ample opportunity to be expressed.

As alluded to previously, a sense of community is hard to achieve in large social institutions. For compassion, empathy, and trust to flourish, organizations need to have a high degree of common identity, which limits the ideal size of such entities to approximately 150 people. From an evolutionary perspective, humans do not have the cognitive capacity to keep relatively detailed social intelligence on more than approximately 150 individuals, or the maximum clan size of our foraging ancestors. Therefore, "clans" consistently outperform larger organizations because they rely primarily on voluntary collaboration instead of compulsory cooperation or compliance.

The good news is that large institutions can gain the same benefits if they reorganize themselves into small, interconnected clusters of people. For example, Asea Brown Boveri (ABB), a global electrical engineering firm, has more than 200 thousand people in its membership. However, each of its approximately five thousand independent operating units around the world consists of an average of only 50 people (a good clan size), and the organization as a whole is linked together through an organic network.

A sense of community is vital because it is the foundation for the voluntary collaboration or social capital needed for the generation of intellectual assets. Janine Nahapiet from the University of Oxford and Sumantra Ghoshal (1998) from the London Business School, in one of the most extensive studies of social and intellectual capital to date, conclude that social capital or a sense of community is based on the interrelationships of three dimensions: structural, relational, and cognitive. "Structural embeddedness concerns the properties of the social system and the network of relationships as a whole [or the community]." Essentially, the structural dimension deals with "the overall pattern of connections between actors—that is, who you reach and how you reach them."

On the other hand, the relational aspect of social capital "focuses on the particular relationships people have, such as respect and friendship, that influence their behavior. It is through these ongoing personal relationships that people fulfill such social motives as sociability, approval, and prestige."

Finally, the cognitive dimension of social capital "refers to those resources providing shared representations, interpretations, and systems of meaning among parties." Basically, all three dimensions further clarify the circular causality inherent in the dynamics of the order parameter or shared identity discussed in Chapter 6. The three dimensions clearly point out the tight coupling of the line-of-sight relationships and sense of community tenets.

Nahapiet and Ghosal (1998) provide two other far-reaching observations about social capital:

> First, as a structural resource, social capital inheres in the relations between persons and among persons. Unlike other forms of capital, social capital is owned jointly by the parties in a relationship, and no one player has or is capable of having exclusive ownership rights. [In addition] . . . social capital cannot be traded easily . . . Second, social capital makes possible the achievement of ends that would be impossible without it or that could be achieved only at extra cost . . . The concept, therefore, is central to the understanding of institutional dynamics, innovation, and value creation.

I might also add that creating high levels of voluntary collaboration is almost impossible without a context (community) where the other-centered, innate human drives are easily expressed and where self-centered drives are minimized. Intimacy, subtlety, and trust must dominate. Accordingly, a close-knit community depends on line-of-sight relationships and positive face-to-face interactions that, in turn, depend on a strong sense of community. Again, we encounter circular causality in action.

COMMON PURPOSE

Defining common purpose is more about philosophy than about dealing with rationale and business information. As Will Durant (1961) said decades ago, "Science without philosophy, facts without perspective and valuation, cannot save us from havoc and despair. Science gives us knowledge, but only philosophy can give us wisdom." Common purpose is about people, their feelings, hopes, aspirations, and perspectives on life in general. It is about meaning and relationships. It is about finding worthwhile strategies for mutual survival.

Attempts to define common purpose without first acknowledging each member in an organization as a partner rather than an employee are almost futile. Defining a common purpose follows the same logic as granting citizenship to members of a democratic society, either by birth or after vigorous screening of immigrants, so that they then have an equal right to vote. Without partnership, how does a firm generate a sense of ownership, agreement, and commitment throughout the workplace? Genuine commitment simply does not happen without these elements, as attested to by the meaningless philosophy and vision statements circulating in most organizations today.

According to Peter Block (1993), in order to have real partnership, four requirements should be present. These requirements include exchange of purpose, right to say "no," joint accountability, and absolute honesty. To begin with, purpose is agreed upon through dialogue, allowing everyone to declare what is to be created. "The same process holds for relationships with customers, suppliers, and other stakeholders. Each has a voice in discussing what the institution will become."

Partners have the right to say "no." "Saying 'no' is the fundamental way we have of differentiating ourselves." To take away someone's right to say "no" is to claim sovereignty over that person. Even though people do not always get what they want, "[they] never lose [their] voice." With the right to say "no" also comes joint accountability. "Each person is responsible for outcomes and the current situation. There is no one else to blame." Being absolutely honest is the final requirement for partnership. Failing to do so "is an act of betrayal. One of the benefits of redistributing power is that people feel less vulnerable and are more honest."

Basically, common purpose encompasses shared values, a sense of self-reference, and a well-developed vision. Common purpose is the DNA or shared meaning of a self-organizing company. Defining shared values is a time-consuming and gut-wrenching process. What emerges from the process, however, is a powerful self-sustaining force that holds an organization together, helping it to take advantage of opportunities that present themselves or to quickly overcome obstacles that arise. Thus, shared values can only be meaningfully defined through consensus involving every member of an enterprise. The process should start at the individual level. Therefore, each associate must first respond to one all-important question: Are my key personal survival needs best satisfied by being or becoming a member of this social institution? People who cannot *honestly* answer this question affirmatively can seldom become *fully* committed to the success of an enterprise because other options will provide considerable distractions away from the need to pursue mutually beneficial goals.

Thus, both individual autonomy and a deep sense of interdependence are essential ingredients for success in a self-organizing entity. Consequently, individual commitments are vital if such a "seemingly" paradoxical system is to function effectively. After all, all biological systems develop and prosper through autonomy and interdependence right down to the molecular level.

Next, organizational members need to answer two more pertinent questions: What do we want to accomplish together? and Who are we trying to serve? These questions, too, are not easily answered. However, what evolves in the process is a persuasive and lasting force that supports noninterference mutualism.

Another look at Figure 4.1 provides an indication of how the answers to the aforementioned three fundamental questions help both categories of our innate drives to be expressed in a balanced manner. That balance, of course, is precisely what the shared values are supposed to help achieve, as is the case with every aspect of all four tenets. Shared-access is about self-interest and mutual-interest, without one impeding the other.

Self-reference, in turn, is like an internal compass that helps each organization member stay on course, even when pursuing individual goals. In other words, it helps people to take a balanced approach between concern for self and concern for others. Therefore, self-reference is closely tied to shared values and vision. Fundamentally, it is the key ingredient for high levels of interdependence, mutuality, and reciprocity, and it is vital for voluntary collaboration.

A shared vision inspires organization members to constantly reach for greater heights and is based on the principle of *creative ten-*

sion. Peter Senge (1990) explains this principle relative to business firms: "Creative tension comes from seeing clearly where we want to be, our 'vision,' and telling the truth about where we are, our 'current reality.' The gap between the two generates a natural tension." Senge's comments point out the importance of not only articulating a desired future but also being acutely aware of the current state of affairs, which heavily depends on the law of requisite variety discussed in the next chapter. In the final analysis, the interactive process used to reach consensus on the common purpose is as important as the results that are attained, and it should be periodically repeated, especially when new people join the organization. For a common purpose to be effective, it needs to fit the frame of reference of every member involved.

VISUALIZING WHOLES

The fourth and final tenet deals with our perceptive capabilities to visualize wholes or engage in systems thinking. The systems view focuses on relationships and integration rather than on individual parts, as is the case in most organizations. Further, "systems thinking is process thinking; form becomes associated with process, interrelation with interaction, and opposites are unified through oscillations," as Fritzof Capra (1982) explains.

Essentially, understanding and developing self-organizing systems are impossible without systems thinking. Fred Kofman and Peter Senge (1993) state: "Rather than thinking of a world of 'parts' that form 'wholes,' we start by recognizing that we live in a world of wholes within wholes. Rather than trying to 'put the pieces together' to make the whole, we recognize that the world is already whole."

A systems view of life not only helps us grasp our relationships with other people and groups, but it also allows us to better understand ourselves and our constant process of transformation. For instance, "whenever we do not take the other as an object for use, whenever we see the other as a legitimate fellow human being with which we can learn and change . . . we engage in a passionate interaction that can open new possibilities for our being," conclude Kofman and Senge. Self-organization starts with individual perceptions; only then is it able to spread throughout an organization. Visualizing wholes is extremely difficult from an organizational perspective without people first sensing that they are equal partners attempting to further the interests of the community as a whole for mutual benefit.

The challenge for business and other social organizations is to appreciate the strengths of the four tenets and design institutions that embrace their bio-logic. A shared-access context is powerful because it nurtures the other-centered human drives without ignoring the self-centered side. It is a cooperative society of friends. Such a context promotes an environment where voluntary collaboration has the best chance to emerge and support the leveraging of intellectual capital. The primary focus of the next chapter is on two powerful dynamic forces emanating from the balanced interplay of the four tenets.

AN EXAMPLE

W.L. Gore & Associates is one of the best examples of how an enterprise can function in the shared-access mode founded on the *Four Tenets for Fostering Human Nature*. I have been extremely impressed by their success and management, or unmanagement, philosophy since I joined Westminster College almost two decades ago. No organization, however, is "perfect," nor will a perfect social institution ever exist. The question that immediately comes to mind is, "Perfect according to whose standards?"

Gore is a privately owned high-technology manufacturing company headquartered in Newark, Delaware, with plants and offices located around the globe. They specialize in the production of unique electronic, medical, fabric, fiber, and filtration products. The company's core competencies are grounded in the intricate use of polytetrafluoroethylene (PTFE), a polymer familiar to most people as DuPont's Teflon. They are best known for discovery of expanded PTFE or GORE-TEX membrane used in outdoor garments and camping equipment. Founded by Genevieve (Vieve) and Wilbert (Bill) Gore in 1958 in the basement of their home, the company has grown to 6,500 associates working in 35 manufacturing locations located around the world, with annual sales of more than one billion dollars.

What is most interesting about Gore is that it was established as a self-organizing system from day one more than 40 years ago. Bill Gore worked for DuPont for 17 years before he and Vieve started their business. They organized the company around "voluntary" teams and believed that people should make their own commitments in relationship to meeting the objectives of the enterprise as a whole. They also thought that these commitments must be taken seriously and that every effort should be made by each associate to keep them. Thus, individual accountability was to one's team members, to whom the commitment was acknowledged as appropriate and important for reaching a business objective.

At Bill's insistence, the Gore organization avoided the use of the word "manager." In fact, Bill Gore is famous for his quotation: "The only person that you manage here is yourself." The emphasis was placed on leadership as opposed to management. Leadership was based on having a following of people who were willing to join an important effort based on their perception of the leader's knowledge, ability, and drive to accomplish a particular business objective.

Consequently, W.L. Gore & Associates has no employees. After one year of service, everyone is a stockholder in an Associate Stock Ownership Plan (ASOP). Except for the title of president, which is required by law, everyone has the same title of "associate." This informal structure gives associates the freedom to define their own career paths and to work where they can use their experience and skills to the maximum advantage of themselves and the enterprise. Bill liked to think of associates "promoting themselves" as they grew in capabilities to contribute to the financial success of the organization.

I remember sitting in Utah Governor Bangerter's office with Bill Gore and some of the Governor's aides in the mid-1980s. Curiously, the Governor asked Bill how many employees he had. With a slight grin, Bill responded, "We have no employees." There was a long pause as Bangerter, obviously confused, tried to digest what Bill had just said. Deliberately taking advantage of the moment, Bill sat in silence to let the tension build until finally, with an even bigger smile, he concluded, "We are all associates!"

Perhaps the most significant operational principle that Bill Gore felt was critical to this company's success was how people communicated. Since no strictly defined hierarchy existed and no titles were used, Gore encouraged associates to go directly to the individual who had the information they needed in order to accomplish a task. He called this concept a "lattice of communication," which meant that anyone could and should go directly to the individual who could help them and not worry about the chain of command. Also, Bill did not want any of the plants to have more than 150 to 200 people to ensure that everyone knew everyone else—a good example of line-of-sight relationships. In fact, I recall how the founder used a bell curve to show why 150 was the maximum optimum size for an organizational unit. Only recently, through my own research, have I been able to determine to my own satisfaction why that limit is important.

Bill looked for new associates to join the organization who were energized by the objectives of the enterprise and who wanted to contribute along the lines of their unique background and skills. He developed the role of "sponsor" to help the new associate get on board and contribute quickly. Sponsoring was not considered a position, but rather an activity by an individual who took an active interest on a one-to-one basis for helping an associate learn how he or she could best impact the business efforts that were being undertaken. In the early phase of employment the sponsor helped the associate begin to formulate his or her own commitments.

Because Gore associates are all part owners, they are reluctant to "waste time" talking to visitors; they have more pressing issues. For example, awhile ago I was invited to spend several days at the three Gore plants in Flagstaff, Arizona. The first morning on site, I was asked to participate (without warning) in a three-hour meeting with one dozen representatives from the plants. This group was finalizing a training package of the four basic operating principles of the company, which I will review shortly. From the moment I was introduced, I was considered a full-fledged group member and was *expected* to participate in the discussion. Continuous heated debate was waged over what the principles really meant and how they should be applied. I was impressed by the extremely open, "no-holds-barred" dialogue among the associates. These discussions were obviously taking place in an atmosphere of trust.

During the same visit, I had an opportunity to spend a few moments with two members of a three-person research team. This team, on their own initiative, had rented an old garage and gas station for their work. When I arrived, they had just been informed of the approval of one of their patents. They also had another patent pending and were working on a third one. I foolishly asked what kinds of schedules they kept. Surprised that I would ask such a question, they replied that they worked until they were completely "drained" (sometimes as long as 24 hours straight). Then they would get some sleep, do some hiking or fishing, and repeat the cycle. These people were obviously very dedicated.

Before I departed, I participated in the deliberations of another team. This 10-person team was trying to determine how to market a new product they had just developed for the dental industry. Interestingly, these people were not marketing experts. Everyone at Gore is essentially organized around specific core competencies. In fact, teams are hesitant to ask assistance from any so-called "experts" other than those within the Gore organization who have a proven track record. Essentially, any kind of administrative "hassle" is avoided as much as possible because it detracts from the real work that they have committed to accomplish.

Gore operates with one guiding objective and four basic principles. The object is simple and profound: "To make money and have fun." Bill saw the "having fun" part as the activity one goes through to "making money." The process of accomplishing the goal should be fun. The principles are equally straightforward. According to Bill Gore (1980), they are:

1. *Fairness.* Each of us will *try* to be fair in all dealings—with each other, with our suppliers, with our customers, within our communities, and with all the people with whom we have transactions or agreements. Fairness is seldom clearly defined, but if a sincere effort is made by all, it generates a tolerance that preserves good feelings among us.
2. *Freedom.* Each of us will allow, help, and encourage his associates to grow in knowledge, skill, the scope of responsibility, and the range of activities. Authority is earned through the power of leadership.
3. *Commitment.* Each of us will make his own commitments—and keep them. No associate can impose a commitment on another.

All commitments are self-commitments. We organize our enterprise—projects, functions, and work of all kinds—through commitments. Therefore, a commitment is a serious matter,
amounting to a contract that must be fulfilled.

4. *Waterline.* Each of us will consult with appropriate associates
   who will share the responsibility of taking any action that has
   the potential of serious harm to the reputation, success, or survival of the enterprise. The analogy is that our enterprise is like a
   ship that we are all in together. Boring holes above the waterline
   is not serious, but below the waterline, holes could sink our
   ship.

In retrospect, I believe Bill Gore was more of a philosopher at
heart than a chemist. Before he passed away unexpectedly in 1986, he
had begun to write a book entitled *Freedom to Dream.* He did not
complete it, but I borrowed several lines from the unpublished manuscript, which I keep as a plaque on the windowsill in my office. It
reads: "The life of each man stands in judgment: Has he dreamed and
followed his dreams so that both his freedom and that of mankind
has advanced by his dreaming?" No wonder W.L. Gore & Associates
leads the pack in generating highly sustained levels of social capital.
They truly know how to unleash human intelligence.

KEY CONSIDERATIONS

- The shift in emphasis from self-centered to other-centered innate
  drives can take place only if we completely *rethink* how social
  systems can and should function. This rethinking requires use of
  bio-logic rather than machine-logic in developing and maintaining our organizations. Rethinking is not about finding new and
  better structures for organizing cooperative endeavors. It is also
  not about discovering a utopian way of social existence that is
  unattainable. Instead, it entails devising the most appropriate
  shared identity for survival in a turbulent environment. Hence,
  what really counts is how an organization takes advantage of its
  "people power" by leveraging information and knowledge
  through a shared-access mode of operation. The resultant posi-

tive emergent social connections that emerge from such a system provide true strategic advantage to an enterprise.

- The Four Tenets for Fostering Human Nature form a *dynamic framework,* giving the other-centered innate drives an opportunity to be expressed but not at the expense of the self-centered drives. As a result, the system as a whole fosters more positive and intense cooperative behavior necessary for the development of knowledge assets. Inherently, the tenets must be *cultivated* into existence because no step-by-step prescription is available, and every social arrangement consists of different people facing different situations. The tenets also overlap and work in a continuously interactive mode, reinforcing each other. Consequently, the system cannot function effectively if one of the tenets is either missing or has not been fully developed. The primary purpose of the tenets is to facilitate the "unleashing" of tacit knowledge through voluntary cooperation. Tacit knowledge can then be made explicit and leveraged for competitive advantage.

REFERENCES

Block, P. (1993) *Stewardship: Choosing Service Over Self-Interest.* Berrett-Koehler, San Francisco, CA, pp. 29–31.

Capra, F. (1982) *The Turning Point.* Simon & Schuster, New York, NY, p. 267.

Covey, S.R. (1989) *The 7 Habits of Highly Effective People.* Simon & Schuster, New York, NY, p. 187.

Durant, W. (1961) *The Story of Philosophy.* Simon & Schuster, New York, NY, p. xxvii.

Ehin, C. (1998) "Fostering Both Sides of Human Nature—The Foundation for Collaborative Relationships," *Business Horizons,* May–June, pp. 15–25.

Ehin, C. (1995) "The Quest for Empowering Organizations: Some Lessons from Our Foraging Past," *Organization Science,* November–December, pp. 666–671.

Fletcher, J.K. (1996) "A Relational Approach to the Protean Worker," in Douglas T. Hall and Associates, *The Career Is Dead—Long Live the Career."* Jossey-Bass, San Francisco, CA, pp.115–124.

Gore, V. (1980) "Policies," W.L. Gore & Associates internal memorandum, November 19, pp. 2–3.

Gore, W.L. (Undated) *Freedom to Dream.* Unpublished manuscript, p. 25.

Hallowell, E.M. (1999) "The Human Moment at Work," *Harvard Business Review*, January–February, pp. 58–66.

Homans, G. (1950) *The Human Group.* Harcourt Brace, New York, NY, pp. 33–40.

Keidel, R.W. (1994) "Rethinking Organizational Design," *Academy of Management Executives*, Vol. 8, No. 4, pp. 12–20.

Kiernan, M.J. (1993) "The New Strategic Architecture: Learning to Compete in the Twenty-first Century," *Academy of Management Executives*, Vol. 7, No. 1, pp. 7–21.

Nahapiet, J. and Ghoshal, S. (1998) "Social Capital, Intellectual Capital, and the Organizational Advantage," *The Academy of Management Review*, March, pp. 242–266.

Nicholson, N. (1997) "Evolutionary Psychology: Toward a New View of Human Nature and Organizational Society," *Human Relations*, Vol. 50, No. 9, pp.1053–1078.

Polanyi, M. (1958) *Personal Knowledge: Towards a Post-Critical Philosophy.* University of Chicago Press, Chicago, IL, pp. 112, 123.

Senge, P. (1990) "The Leader's New Work: Building Learning Organizations," *Sloan Management Review*, Fall, pp. 7–23.

Spreitzer, G. (1996) "Social Structural Characteristics of Psychologic Empowerment," *Academy of Management Journal*, April, Vol. 39(2), pp. 485–504.

Stewart, T.A. (1997) *Intellectual Capital: The New Wealth of Organizations.* Doubleday/Currency, New York, NY, pp. 70–73.

Sveiby, K.E. (1997) *The New Organizational Wealth: Managing & Measuring Knowledge-Based Assets.* Berrett-Koehler, San Francisco, CA, pp. 31, 37.

6

Getting Started

*To achieve the marvelous, it is precisely the
unthinkable that must be thought.*

Tom Robbins

Firms that develop their affairs based on the logic outlined in the previous chapter will steadfastly outperform organizations intent on
continuing to "fine tune" existing hierarchical structures, no matter
how flat they become. Adopting the formal self-organizing mode allows companies to leverage information and knowledge much more
effectively in two unique ways: The self-organizing mode involves (1)
an *order parameter* or shared identity that cannot be imitated and (2)
adherence to the *law of requisite variety*, which stipulates that organizational complexity must match environmental complexity.

THE ORDER PARAMETER

Another look at Figure 5.1 in the previous chapter shows that the order parameter is located in the region where all the tenets overlap.
The order parameter is a dynamic yet synergistic property of a system that depends on the continuous interaction of the four tenets.
Recall that Haken (1981) suggested that the order parameter is created by the cooperation of autonomous members of a system who
constantly experiment with new mutually beneficial positions and reaction processes. As better methods and processes emerge through

continual member interaction with internal and external environments of the system, they are immediately incorporated into the order parameter.

In turn, the order parameter provides dynamic stability or *shared identity* to the system by influencing the behavior of the individual members and groups. Order is an "invisible hand" that keeps the system together by achieving coordination without control. Essentially, the order parameter facilitates the continual leveraging of information and knowledge without interfering with the activities and interactions of the independent members of the organization.

The order parameter is akin to the improvisation of a jazz band. The band consists of highly skilled musicians who are capable of both leading or following, depending on the situation. A common theme or melody is present, but what develops is strictly based on *emergent properties* (tacit knowledge) that evolve among the band members and their audience. No score or director is followed. The music that emerges, however, is powerful and unique to the situation.

In addition, constant practice by the musicians individually and as a group develops their proficiency even further and raises their improvisation skills to even greater heights. No limit can be put on the complexity of improvisations that a jazz band or a shared-access organization can attain, and these emerging properties cannot be imitated. Lack of slick or quick duplication is the ultimate in strategic advantage.

The vital interrelationships of the four tenets, whether in a jazz group or an organization, can easily be seen. Without the interplay of the tenets, improvisation or positive emergent cooperative behavior has little chance of developing. Fully engaged, however, the tenets provide a context that supports an almost limitless array of possibilities and actions because the other-centered drives also have a chance to be expressed.

Clearly, the order parameter or shared identity has nothing in common with "groupthink" or "country club" relationships. Groupthink restrains creativity by demanding conformity. In a country club setting, everyone has a good time for him or herself with little consideration given to cooperative endeavors. The order parameter depends on both individual autonomy and a deep sense of group interdependence simultaneously. Both goals need to be pursued in a balanced fashion in order for the synergistic power of the order parameter to be set in motion. Once more, we observe the potency of circular causality of biological systems.

As previously stipulated, the shared-access context is not for the faint of heart. Rather, it is reserved for people who are able and willing to raise their survival skills to continuously higher levels through bio-logic. Ultimately, the order parameter is the *binding and propelling force* emanating from the interplay of the four tenets, which support both individual and cooperative efforts simultaneously.

REQUISITE VARIETY

Being able to adhere very closely to the law of requisite variety gives a self-organizing system an additional advantage over its conventional hierarchical counterparts. The law of requisite variety is a systems theory concept introduced by W.R. Ashby (1956) in the 1950s. This law stipulates that for a system to properly survive, it must be capable of matching whatever complexity its environment presents. As Ashby puts it, "*only variety can destroy variety.*"

Clearly, matching environmental variables on a one-to-one basis is the ideal in attaining requisite variety. That match, however, is seldom possible in a typical company setting. Therefore, most firms develop variety only for those factors with a high probability of occurrence and pay little attention to the rest. Although companies could get away with this haphazard matching in the past, it is not a smart strategy for today's increasingly unpredictable world.

Information clearly plays a vital role in dealing with requisite variety. Hence, organizations better able to scan the environment and disseminate acquired information to *all* members, so they can individually or in teams respond as necessary, have a competitive advantage. Here again, the self-organizing shared-access mode looks extremely promising.

Figure 6.1 depicts the requisite variety capability of a typical hierarchical structure. Such a system clearly cannot respond to its environment on a one-to-one basis. Thus, a system is incapable of developing requisite variety because all of the vital information from external and internal sources is first gathered and screened by the

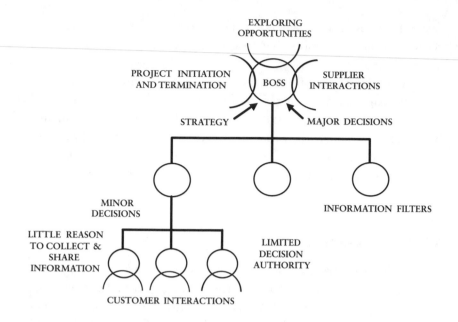

Figure 6.1   *One-to-Many with the Internal and External Environment*

"boss." Subsequently, the boss makes all the major decisions, based on his or her interpretations.

Obviously, the organization is able to react to multiple internal and external demands with only single or limited responses. No matter how brilliant the boss is, and no matter how many "super computers" he or she uses, the firm is still limited to a one-to-many capability in initiating required interactions and activities in dealing with changing conditions. In addition, all external information is "filtered" through one or a limited number of people, which is hardly an efficient way of gathering and interpreting information.

In the past, and still in most organizations today, requisite variety is reduced to manageable levels by means of policies, standard operating procedures, and regulations. In order to reduce uncertainty, these decision rules have been developed to project courses of action based on previous experience and trends. Such an approach has been effective in a relatively slow-changing environment, but it will not suffice in the future, especially in industries where knowledge and intellectual assets are the keys to success. As the intellectual content of work increases, standards become counterproductive because they are incapable of helping people to respond to unanticipated events.

Figure 6.2 presents a different picture. A cursory look reveals that this system clearly has the potential for requisite variety. Sufficient permutation variety in the system provides a one-to-one interchange with the internal and external environment. This figure depicts a classic example of the viability and power of a formal self-organizing system operating in the shared-access mode. First, the organization is capable of coordinating its internal and external activities and interactions without control. No "boss" holds the system together, screens all the information, and makes all the major decisions. Instead, the system is constantly poised for action and kept on course by its shared vision, the constant exchange of *all* information, and an *evolving strategy* that continuously matches environmental demands and internal capabilities. The system is poised to handle any unanticipated situation in real time.

Second, every member of the firm is not only aware of internal needs but is also in constant contact with his or her immediate external stakeholders. Information and knowledge are endlessly shared

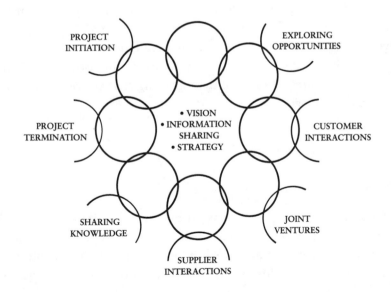

Figure 6.2 *One-to-One with the Internal and External Environment*

without first having to be screened by anyone. The system is in a per-petual one-to-one relationship with its members and the environ-ment. It has the requisite variety necessary to respond properly to changing environmental conditions. This type of organization is ide-ally suited for the Knowledge Age because it provides a context that nurtures the other-centered drives to the fullest extent possible and supports voluntary collaborative relationships needed for leveraging intellectual capital.

USING BIO-LOGIC

Imagine that you are the president of a medium-sized software com-pany. Until recently, your firm has grown 15 to 20 percent annually in sales. During the past year, however, your sales figures have shown a significant slump. What do you do to get back on track? Most likely, you appoint a project leader who identifies and asks key indi-viduals in the firm with cross-functional expertise to join his or her team to analyze the problem(s) and make recommendations about the proper course(s) of action. You probably also ask an outside consul-tant for advice and to work with the project team. Finally, the odds are high that you appoint a steering committee composed of your top vice presidents and directors to monitor the actions of the problem-solving team and to screen their recommendations.

In most instances, the primary focus of this problem-solving/change process are one or all of the following four conventional orga-nizational elements:

1. Technology
2. Products and services
3. Administration
4. Human resource management

Fundamentally, everyone assembled to arbitrate what needs to be done first tries to determine if certain types of hardware (e.g., computers, machinery) and work processes are the key candidates for change. Next, modifications to existing products and services or the possible introduction of some new products and services are scru-tinized. Third, the company's mission, structure, culture, and management style are thoroughly analyzed. Last but not least, employees' skills, training, rewards, and motivation receive ample attention. In some instances, all four elements may even be targeted at the same time.

What are the probable results? Success at an acceptable level but with marginal overall effect on the organization in the long run. Granted, the people trying to solve the problem are experienced, creative, and hard-working individuals. Therefore, the problem(s) is solved at least temporarily or until another team, consultant, and steering committee has to be assembled to put out another "fire." Or, as Chris Argyris (1994) stated: ". . . it is possible to achieve quite respectable productivity with middling commitment and morale . . . In such a system, superficial answers to critical questions produce adequate results, and no one demands more."

The predicament here and in most organizations is that everyone involved is trying to effect meaningful change without any appreciable change in thinking or rethinking. In other words, think, act, and interact the same way and you always attain the same results. Basically, everyone concerned is using machine-logic consciously or unconsciously. The thinking is, "How can we fix the organization (machine) so that its behavior (function) can be properly controlled to ensure acceptable sales (output)?" Again, we are confusing control with order and machines with people.

Instead, we should be looking for guidance from the biological world where order *emerges* from chaos through self-organization in the pursuit of common goals. Such order is dynamic and constantly self-adjusting in response to changing conditions. Thus, rather than trying to devise better control mechanisms, the objective should be to develop social systems that are self-reviewing and self-correcting. In such systems, people learn to organize themselves in an infinite variety of ways by continuously expanding the choices available to the organization (requisite variety) as it copes with the demands of a changing environment.

Essentially, in the Knowledge Age, concentrating on the four conventional organizational elements just summarized provides a firm with minimal competitive advantage. Rather, a company's change effort should primarily focus on the following four vital self-organizing elements:

1. Organizational context
2. Social and intellectual wherewithal
3. Order-parameter
4. Requisite variety

Organizational members should first identify in what type of an organizational context they currently function to see how well all the human innate drives have a chance to be expressed in a balanced fashion. That goal can be accomplished with the aid of Box 4.1, Identifying the Controlled-Access Context, and Box 4.2, Identifying the Shared-Access Context.

Second, Figure 5.1 should be used to determine the levels of social and intellectual assets present in the firm. What needs to be discovered is whether the organization is a tightly knit "clan" with a common purpose where tacit knowledge is freely shared in the pursuit of practical, innovative ideas. Third, again using Figure 5.1, associates should determine the presence and strength of a common identity providing dynamic order. That is, how strong is the binding and propelling invisible force emanating from the four overlapping tenets that support both individual and cooperative efforts simultaneously. Finally, using Figures 6.1 and 6.2, the organization needs to discover its environmental-scanning capabilities. The company should be adept at continuously identifying the worldwide forces affecting its competitiveness and sharing that information with its members to amplify the requisite variety of the entire system.

The intent is to ensure that all the activities, interactions, and sentiments in self-organizing entities are grounded on the balanced expression of both the self-centered and other-centered innate human drives. As Alfie Kohn (1992) postulates, "One of the most powerful motivators is not money or victory but a sense of accountability to others. This is precisely what cooperation establishes: the knowledge that others are dependent on you." In essence, circular causality brings about emergent order as tacit knowledge percolates to the surface. In other words, act, think, and interact differently, and in the process you get different and more meaningful results. Chapter 7 describes in detail a comprehensive model for managing knowledge organizations. It shows the vital links among social capital, intellectual capital, and market responsiveness.

GETTING STARTED

More specifically, in order to get started in developing organizations that are founded on the four tenets for fostering human nature, or bio-logic, social institutions must lay a strong foundation composed of four critical components. First, work processes need to be arranged into "clans" of no more than 150 people for reasons outlined earlier. Obviously, in large firms, these "communities" would be part of a closely knit, worldwide network that, when necessary, can support any member of the web with its vast total resources.

Organizing these clans functionally, such as sales, engineering, research and development, and so forth, as we are still accustomed to doing is illogical. Rather, these intricate communities should be formed around unique *dynamic core competencies*. Core competencies must not be confused with businesses and products. Both businesses and products are founded on core competencies.

In their seminal work, "The Core Competencies of the Corporation," C.K. Prahalad and Gary Hamel (1990) define core competencies as "the collective learning in organizations, especially how to coordinate diverse production skills and integrate multiple streams of technologies." One of the primary reasons that clans should be formed around core competencies is that core competencies do not depreciate with use. "Unlike physical assets, which do deteriorate over time, competencies are enhanced as they are applied and shared," conclude Prahalad and Hamel. Circular causality is at work again.

Prahalad and Hamel recommend three tests for the identification of core competencies. "First, a core competence provides potential access to a wide variety of markets . . . Second, a core competence should make a significant contribution to the perceived customer benefits of the end product . . . Finally, a core competence should be difficult for competitors to imitate." They also suggest that few firms can develop more than five or six world-class fundamental competencies. In other words, an organization (as well as individuals) needs to "discover" what they are genuinely good at in order to take advantage of those inherent predispositions.

Essentially, innovative products and services are the by-products of dynamic core competencies, which can be categorized into three general areas of collective learning: (1) expertise in certain technologies, (2) coordination or process skills, and (3) special abilities in developing and maintaining external relationships or networks (Mascarenhas, Baveja, and Jamil, 1998). Exceptional technological expertise is based on a thorough understanding of a specific field of knowledge. Thus, it requires an intimate grasp of the latest developments in that area and continuous experimentation with the properties involved in order to improve or discover new characteristics of those properties. Of course, the acquired technologies must be capable of being put to practical use and be of greater value than those of competitors around the world. Dependable processes can include the capability to rapidly transfer skills from one location to another, coordination of activities to satisfy unique customer requirements, or consistency in obtaining expeditious approval from regulatory agencies. Fundamentally, sustained success in this area and technological know-how depends primarily on high levels of social capital or voluntary collaboration.

Finally, close relationships with external constituencies provide another vital source for organizational success. For instance, customers, suppliers, distributors, state and federal agencies, and so on can provide tremendous assistance for the maintenance and development of the other two core competencies. They constitute the "external" social capital of an enterprise. Margaret Wheatly (1992) succinctly describes the overall benefits of core competencies to an organization:

> A business that focuses on its core competencies identifies itself as a portfolio of skills rather than as a portfolio of business units. It can respond quickly to new opportunities because it is not locked into the rigid boundaries of pre-established end products or businesses. Such an organization is both sensitive to its environment and resilient from it. In deciding on products and markets, it is guided internally by its competencies, not just the attractiveness or difficulty of a particular market.

Clans also need to function through the interplay of "free-flowing" teams—essentially, teams where membership is voluntary and whose members are usually participating in several team projects at a time. As Eric Matson (1998) of the *Los Angeles Times Syndicate* makes clear, "In the past, people focused on their direct relationship with their manager. In a project environment people need strong healthy relationships with their peers." The main consideration here is narrowing the gap between unchanging human nature and the present-day organizational context. To decrease this gap, people need opportunities for both autonomy (choice) and voluntary collaboration in pursuit of common interests.

Second, members of a clan must have an opportunity to "overtly" participate in developing and continuously updating the internal and external context in which they work. Unless we insist on using machine-logic, the organizational change process *cannot* be left to pilot teams, consultants, and steering committees. No matter how well intended, such groups are incapable of taking everyone's perspectives into consideration. Without opportunities to voice their views based on their selective categorization of organizational problems and opportunities, the other-centered drives of clan members will seldom be expressed.

Involving everyone in running an organization may seem to you like a charming idea that is much too utopian to be practical in real life. Not so. In fact, such democratic work principles date back to 1951 when social scientists Eric Trist and Fred Emery began to study self-organizing work teams at the Haigmoor South Yorkshire British Coal Mine. Later, with the help of his wife Merrelyn, Emery formulated a new method for creating actively adaptive, democratic workplaces, which he named *participative design*. According to Emery (Hamson et al., 1997):

> The expert driven change methodologies (such as re-engineering) contrive the tired old concept of designing the technical system first and force-fitting the social system into it. Once the responsibility is put back where the work is done, people themselves will take responsibility for making the technical system work. That means you change the social structure of work first and as a result everything else changes.

The Emerys' participative design concept is based on six human requirements for productive work that also seem to complement the four broader tenets for fostering human nature. These six requirements include the following:

1. Adequate elbow room for decision making
2. Opportunity to learn continuously on the job
3. An optimum level of variety
4. Mutual support and respect
5. Meaningfulness
6. A desirable future (personal growth and increase in skills)

The most fascinating part of participative design is that people can begin to apply the six principles *on their own* after a two- to three-day seminar conducted by a participative design workshop expert. My friend and international consultant, Frank Heckman, sums it up best (Heckman, 1997):

> Since the 1950s when Trist stumbled upon this group of coal miners at the Haigmoor, the methods for creating productive democratic organizations has been well developed by Fred and Merrelyn Emery and their colleagues around the world. What is really encouraging and exciting is that more and more people today are beginning to discover, including complexity theorists, that democracy is not a political agenda but an integral part of the natural order of things and is perhaps the most sensible way to achieve the best attainable solutions among conflicting practical, political, and moral interests!

The key to success in using the participative design concept or any other meaningful change process is that it must be initiated from the start by internal constituents of an organization who are directly impacted by the proceedings. Consultants can facilitate the process and provide the fundamental principles to be applied; however, they will never be fully part of the shared-access self-organizing system that needs to emerge and mature because no matter how deeply involved they are, they will eventually leave. Accordingly, what happens to the interrelationships or circular causalities that have evolved over time when they depart? They are severed, of course, and new interrelationships have to be developed or the system reverts back to its former routines.

Typically, pilot programs, experimental teams, steering committees, and others have the same effect. Again, what happens to the web of relationships that has been formed when these groups are disbanded? Self-organization is an emergent process that does not take place overnight. It requires time, effort, and dedication. Thus, an effective team or clan depends on relatively stable relationships. Therefore, even in today's turbulent environment, we still need some constancy.

More important, social stability is indispensable for sharing tacit knowledge. Expertise (tacit knowledge that we can never fully access and articulate) cannot be transferred from one person or group to another by formal means such as seminars, training manuals, books, and e-mail. Each person builds up his or her own expertise over time by selective categorization (discussed in Chapter 3). Hence, close relationships that allow the other-centered innate human drives to be expressed provide the proper context for "rubbing shoulders" with other knowledgeable people; in the process, tacit knowledge is made explicit and public. The resultant explicit knowledge can then be distributed, analyzed, and added to individual and organizational core competencies. In turn, this formal knowledge triggers more tacit knowledge and the cycle continues.

One more vital point needs to be discussed concerning member involvement in the clan change process—open-book management. For shared-access to work and for balanced expression of innate human drives to take place, "secrets" cannot be kept among clan members. That includes sharing of all financial and operating information with everyone. Therefore, three things need to take place if people are going to be truly considered as associates and partners.

First, people need to not only have free access to financial statements, but they must also be trained to read them. Second, everyone should be capable of linking his or her work to the organization's financial results. That is, every individual and team needs to be able to see how much value they are adding to the firm both for the determination of productivity and for basic compensation. Finally, to one degree or another, everyone should share in the ownership of the organization. That means during good years, associates determine how much of the profits should be reinvested and how much should be distributed among the clan members. The same rules apply to lean years—everyone suffers equitably in the losses.

For example, Bill Gross (1998), the founder and chairman of Idealab (his previous companies include GNP Development and Knowledge Adventure), has consistently proven that giving all members of a firm *significant* equity ownership in the organization (where the equity potential dwarfs their salary) magnifies human involvement and innovation more than the financial potential may suggest. He has dubbed this type of equity sharing the "new math of ownership." Gross stipulates that:

> . . . the multiplicative effect of setting employees free and giving them significant equity has a net positive result. It's a counterintuitive arithmetic, one that I came to embrace despite myself. But I decided to put this arithmetic—this notion of relinquishing ownership and of letting go—at the very heart of a new venture.

The good news is that more companies are opening their books and providing their members with an overall stake in the welfare of their enterprises.

The third fundamental part of getting started in developing a shared-access context is involving all clan members in answering the three critical questions posed in Chapter 5. These questions are as follows:

1. Are my personal survival needs best satisfied by being or becoming a member of this social institution? (personal-level question)
2. What do we want to accomplish together? (clan-level question)
3. Who are we trying to serve? (clan-level question)

Again, these questions are deep and "emotional" and not easily answered. They are, however, key to the establishment of relationships firmly based on interdependence, mutuality, reciprocity, and trust.

In order to begin to answer these three questions, we must first remember that life processes at both the individual and group levels center around the management of scarce resources needed for survival and the perpetuation of genes. The survival mode includes seeking as much satisfaction as possible from our journey through life. That is why we desire novelty and pleasure. Our creative skills and our ability to entertain and to be entertained are vital parts of our survival framework. As mentioned earlier, these abilities and desires make life enjoyable and meaningful, motivating us to pursue increasingly higher and more fulfilling goals. We all require various levels of motivation for survival. Therefore, from an organizational perspective, the answers to the three questions must address not only everyone's basic physiological needs but also overall contentment with life in general. How else can both sides of human nature be fostered for competitive advantage?

Finally, established organizations that are functioning in a controlled-access mode but that want to change to a shared-access context initially require committed, visionary leadership to start the process. Such leadership has several names, but they all have essentially the same meaning. Peter Senge calls these types of individuals "servant leaders" who are willing to devote their efforts to serving others in achieving common goals. Peter Block, on the other hand, refers to these people as "stewards" who focus their energies on guiding others into becoming responsible team players.

These transformational leaders have two extremely important tasks to accomplish. One is to make a firm determination that the organization will transition to a shared-access mode of operation and that it will not turn back. The leaders must then show by constant word and deed that they really mean what they have promised to bring about.

From the beginning, these leaders also need to openly declare that their primary task is to work themselves out of their *assigned* positions of power. This transition will take place gradually as everyone within an organization becomes more involved, willing, and able to assume responsibility and accountability for the activities of the clan and the associated total institutional network. This transition does not mean that the stewards or servants will eventually be required to leave the organization; they will simply work in different capacities as partners voluntarily collaborating with other members of the firm for mutually beneficial results, as is the case with everyone in the community.

Leadership will not disappear from the organizational landscape. Rather, it should become *situational* and distributed throughout the social system, emerging serendipitously at appropriate occasions as people working together encounter unexpected problems and opportunities. Such leadership will be founded on knowledge, experience, and persuasion skill, and not on position and reward power.

Human beings have lived without chiefs or bosses for 200 thousand years and for millions of years before that as we evolved into *Homo sapiens*. We are born as complete self-organizing systems. Controlling machines makes sense; however, trying to control the behavior of people creates negative and unpredictable consequences. For instance, showing a child how to cross a busy street by holding his or her hand for the first few times makes a lot of sense. Holding the child's hand for the rest of his or her life makes no sense at all, and interferes with growth.

We need to take advantage of human nature instead of trying to control it. As Eric Klein and John Izzo (1998), co-authors of *Awakening Corporate Soul*, postulate, "The Path of Community is based on the realization that a fundamental interdependence underlies everything we do. Every service rendered or product delivered is the result of an incalculable cooperative effort. We really are in this together." We will always need situational leadership, but relying on chiefs and bosses is dangerous, especially when success depends on the creation and application of new ideas.

SOME CLOSING OBSERVATIONS

Developing a shared-access context based on the four tenets for fostering human nature is not for everyone. The system requires conscientious and dedicated people willing to work as partners. Companies where the intellectual content of work is high and getting higher are ultimately best suited to implementing a shared-access context. Without understanding and properly supporting the expression of innate human drives, however, knowledge companies have little chance of surviving in the future. People simply cannot be forced to be creative and innovative. Fresh ideas come from committed individuals and teams because minds cannot be "supervised."

Is this idea of genuine partnership merely a "pipe dream," or have organizations actually applied the ideas I've proposed? Many companies are developing human-friendly systems, and the number continues to grow. Recent studies indicate that organizations now seem to grasp that many people want to apply their knowledge and skills voluntarily at work, desire more autonomy on their jobs, and want to contribute to business decisions. Firms need, however, to get a better grasp of human nature.

If you would like to read about examples of organizations that have begun to use the self-organizing mode extensively, I suggest you consult Thomas Petzinger's (1999) latest book, *The New Pioneers*. He studied companies in 40 cities in the United States as well as businesses from abroad, and he presents many examples throughout his book. Some of the leading companies progressively moving in the shared-access direction include ABB (mentioned before), Rowe Furniture, Koch Industries, Technical and Computer Graphics in Australia, Semco in Brazil, and Southwest Airlines. As presented in the previous chapter, one company stands above the rest—W.L. Gore & Associates. Ironically, they have been operating in a formal self-organizing mode for approximately 40 years.

My long-time friend, John Giovale, succinctly conveys why W.L. Gore & Associates have been so successful from his own experience with the company (Ehin, 1995):

> When I started at W.L. Gore & Associates, Inc., nearly 28 years ago, the company was considered odd. There were no titles, employees referred to themselves as associates, there were sponsors instead of bosses. Associates were encouraged to make their own commitments. Critics from outside of Gore believed that such a structure could not survive substantial growth. Over the last 20 years, however, Gore has grown in revenues at the rate of 26 percent per year; many companies are attempting to emulate Gore's structure and operating principles.

I believe that *any* social system is capable of formally self-organizing with proper support and training. Such organizations have a much greater potential for stimulating innovation, increasing productivity, and promoting high levels of individual and group responsibility. Above all, these organizations are extremely responsive and flexible in meeting constantly changing conditions. What other choice do we have since streamlining or flattening our hierarchical systems is not creating the desired results? In fact, extensive research by noted academicians Jeffrey Pfeffer and John Veiga (1999) indicates that current "organizations often inadvertently destroy wisdom and competence or make it impossible for wisdom, knowledge, and experience to benefit the firm." The importance of tacit knowledge again comes to the fore.

Although the shared-access approach is by no means perfect, I know of no better option. "For the world of our own making has become so complicated that we must turn to the world of the born to understand how to manage it. That is, the more mechanical we make our fabricated environment, the more biological it will eventually have to be if it is to work at all" (Kelly, 1994). In the end, business in the future is all about perceptions and rethinking. After all, the mind interacts more with itself than anything else. There *is* hope for democracy in the workplace. We have social brains that have evolved to the present state for many thousands of years. We come equipped for making positive and lasting social connections, given the proper conditions. Why else does *every* culture in the world have something like the "Golden Rule"? Next, I provide a total systems perspective for leveraging intellectual capital.

EXAMPLES

I have decided to use three cases instead of just one to better convey why the key organizational considerations presented in this chapter are most appropriate for managing change in the Knowledge Age. Sometimes comparing and contrasting several approaches is more appropriate than a straight narrative of one situation. In following these examples, try to recall the points I have emphasized concerning the order parameter (shared identity), requisite variety, dynamic core competencies, and effecting "meaningful" needed change.

Synergy Unlimited, or SU (a pseudonym), is a publicly held company generating close to half a billion dollars in annual revenues. It is a multinational firm known for conducting seminars designed to increase individual and organizational leadership abilities, trust, and productivity. SU also produces and sells the necessary products to support the services they provide.

In the last couple years, overall SU sales have stayed relatively flat and have even fallen in some areas of operations. As a result, investors have begun to lose confidence and company stock has steadily declined. Thus, SU is clearly a leading candidate for a buy-out. What has the firm's general response been to this obviously deteriorating condition? Essentially, to fine-tune their existing products and services (even adding some state-of-the-art technology), to reorganize a little and move some people around, and to ask their people to work harder.

It does not take a genius to determine that doing the same thing better and harder is not going to solve the problem. Investors are looking for innovative products and services that respond to the continuously changing global markets. SU's core competencies have apparently ceased to be dynamic. Put another way, their core competencies have become *core rigidities*. That condition is a corporate "disease" that is usually fatal in the Knowledge Era. Without taking appropriate risks and drastically rethinking, SU will not be able to survive in its current form.

How can a company that prides itself in delivering leadership, team, and productivity enhancement seminars all over the world not heed its own advice? Unfortunately, this predicament is common, especially for large and formerly successful enterprises. Fundamentally, they have not only lost the *requisite variety* to sustain themselves in a changing environment, but they have also lost the flexibility to take quick, decisive action to find and seize new opportunities.

My business partner and I have had several discussions with three very astute vice presidents of SU. Each time, however, we have departed shaking our heads in disbelief. During the initial meeting with one of the vice presidents, we were told that my model for generating, capturing, and leveraging intellectual capital (discussed in Chapter 7) was probably a good idea, but that they were too busy right now trying to sell their existing products and services. Besides, they were already doing something "very similar" (the dreaded "not-invented-here" syndrome). Our meeting and subsequent telephone conversations with the other two executives proved to be equally interesting. Surprisingly, my model received considerable enthusiastic attention after we signed several proprietary disclosure forms. My partner and I wondered for a long time after the meeting what we could have or would have wanted to "steal" from SU.

We first asked them if they had considered focusing on the knowledge management business since conducting various training seminars was their livelihood. The initial response was that they were "kind of" in that business already. Subsequently, they reluctantly admitted that they really were not focused on "intellectual capital" per se even after showing a brand new product they had just developed. What an irony, I thought, as we continued our discussion. Decades ago, the railroad industry, thinking they were in the railroad instead of the transportation business, almost vanished when trucks and planes came along. Here at the dawn of the twenty-first century, SU thinks they are in the seminar rather than the knowledge business and thus seem to be repeating history.

After we presented the details of my model, the executives told us that they would get back to us in several weeks after reviewing it with their "boss" and two other colleagues. Also, even if the proposal turned out to be "the goose that laid the golden eggs," it would not be considered for implementation for at least another year. What we discovered was that, even at the executive level, no one at SU wanted to take a stand or voice a personal opinion. It soon became apparent that decisions (at least in this division) were made by complete consensus. For instance, our proposal was turned down because one out of the five people who reviewed it felt it was too much of a "rehash" of known concepts.

Most disturbing, this bastion of trust and interdependence is an extremely closed system. People everywhere are cordial, almost to the point of being reverent, but a strong sense of hierarchical subservience hangs in the air. If you want to talk to anybody who is considered to be a high-level decision maker, you have to penetrate several impregnable guarded gates that are seldom even cracked open. Hence, they are literally incapable of seeing an opportunity even when it stares them squarely in the face.

For instance, I wanted to make an informal luncheon date with one of the founders whom I had personally known when he first started the business. I was "grilled" by his administrative assistant as to "exactly" why I wanted to see him. I responded that I wanted to have an informal chat to exchange ideas with him. Reluctantly, she finally agreed to make an appointment for the meeting in approximately four months if I would first provide her with a "talking paper" for the occasion. I think I could get an audience with a king or queen faster than that. What is missing at SU is a moat with a drawbridge around their office complex. How can the two founders possibly know what is happening in the trenches? Even considering an order parameter or shared identity is illogical in such an organization. Practicing "ostrichism" is deadly in today's discontinuous environment.

Large companies are not the only ones that lack requisite variety and the ability to focus on what is most important. Best Systems, or BS (a pseudonym), is a small high-technology company with considerable expertise in the field of wireless communications. It employs approximately one dozen people and has been in existence for around three years. Unfortunately, it has yet to make a profit.

Two years ago, one of the company's major investors asked me to speak to the CEO to see if I could provide some guidance for improving the firm's operations. Enthusiastically, I approached the CEO and offered him my assistance. I was shown every detail of the organization and introduced to most of its people. The company clearly possessed some unique core competencies, primarily due to the expertise of the individual in charge of research and development (the organization is primarily R&D-based).

After the initial tour, instead of being asked to point out problems and possible opportunities, I was invited to develop a vision and organizational structure for the establishment. Scratching my head, I departed. When I returned a week or so later, I gave the CEO a framework to use for generating a vision with his team. Further, I suggested that he focus on selecting only several key products to work on and market rather than relying on a "product of the week" scheme that had yet to produce concrete results. I also suggested that he find a more suitable job for the marketing person who had yet to conduct any marketing research but kept "promising the moon" to every potential customer. Finally, I recommended that his entire organization (12 people) could be molded into a productive self-managing team with some training and facilitation. That structure would create the focus that they badly needed.

I don't believe he heard anything I said, although he appeared attentive and kept hanging onto my every word. First, he responded that he could not move or "offend" the marketing person because he owned too much stock, which he was initially given as an incentive to join the company. What really startled me was that he next asked me how many divisions the organization needed to run effectively. "Divisions? You have just the right size for a self-managing team. What do you need divisions for?" I responded and left shortly thereafter. The man obviously wanted to run a fiefdom. Paradoxically, the company still exists, although it still has not generated any income. Shared identity? They have no idea in what direction they are going even on a daily basis.

The two previous cases are quite a contrast from Rowe Furniture Company as reported by Thomas Petzinger (1999). Situated in the Appalachian foothills of western Virginia, Rowe furniture was run like a typical assembly-line sweatshop for 40 years, producing quality furniture for showrooms across the United States. In the mid-1990s, the market changed. Furniture buyers suddenly wanted custom-designed products, and they were not about to wait more than three months for delivery.

As luck would have it, the company hired a new manufacturing chief for the plant to develop a "hyperefficient assembly process." However, the new chief had other ideas from day one. Instead of developing ways to make the assembly line faster and more efficient, she abandoned it altogether. Most supervisory positions disappeared, and the 500 workers assembled into clusters or cells. Each team was given responsibility for a particular line of products, and *they* designed their own processes and procedures around them. Each team also had real-time access to all the information they needed—orders, output, and productivity and quality data. Thus, they knew exactly which of their actions worked or did not.

Confusion reigned for several weeks, but then the pieces began to fall in place and order appeared out of chaos. Productivity and quality went sky high. In no time, deliveries were made in 30 days and shortly thereafter in only 10 days—an unbelievable accomplishment in an industry where lead times could be as long as six months. Unmanagement or self-organization can unleash human potential "even" in a furniture factory; it only requires courage and determination, but it can also produce high margins.

KEY CONSIDERATIONS

- The order parameter or shared identity is a dynamic yet synergistic property of a system that depends on the continuous interaction of the four tenets. It is created by the cooperation of autonomous members of a tightly knit network who constantly experiment with new mutually beneficial positions and reaction processes. As better methods and processes emerge through this continual member interaction with the internal and external environments of the system, they are then immediately incorporated into the order parameter. The order parameter also provides dynamic stability to the system by influencing the behavior of the individual members and groups. It is an "invisible hand" that keeps a system together by achieving coordination without control. Essentially, the order parameter facilitates the continual leveraging of information and knowledge without interfering with the activities and interactions of the independent organization members. It depends on both individual autonomy and a deep sense of group interdependence simultaneously.

- Being able to adhere closely to the law of requisite variety gives a self-organizing system an additional advantage over its conventional hierarchical counterpart. The law simply stipulates that for a system to properly survive, it must match whatever complexity its environment presents. Matching environmental variables on a one-to-one basis is the ideal in attaining requisite variety, and only self-organizing systems have the capability of achieving and sustaining that level of diversification. Information clearly plays a vital role in dealing with requisite variety. Hence, organizations that are better able to scan the environment and disseminate acquired information to *all* members, so they can respond as necessary individually or in teams, have a competitive advantage.

- In order to get started in developing organizations that are founded on the four tenets, a social institution must lay a strong foundation composed of four critical components. First, work processes need to be arranged into "clans" of no more than 150 people for reasons outlined earlier. These clans should be formed around unique dynamic core competencies and not functional specialties. Also, these clans need to be composed of autonomous but interdependent, voluntary, free-flowing teams. Second, all members of this small community must have an opportunity to take part in developing and continuously updating the internal and external context in which they work. This process cannot be left to pilot projects, consultants, and steering committees. Third, all clan members need to answer the following three questions:

1. Are my personal survival needs best satisfied by being or becoming a member of this social institution?
2. What do we want to accomplish together?
3. Who are we trying to serve?

Finally, established organizations that are functioning in a controlled-access mode but that want to change to a shared-access context initially require dedicated, committed, and visionary leadership to start the process. However, from the beginning of the change process, these leaders need to *openly* declare that their primary task is to work themselves out of their *assigned* positions of power.

REFERENCES

Ashby, W.R. (1956) *An Introduction to Cybernetics.* Chapman and Hall, London, England, pp. 206–218.

Ehin, C. (1995) "The Ultimate Advantage of Self-Organizing Systems," *Journal of Quality and Participation*, September, pp. 30–38.

Gross, B. (1998) "The New Math of Ownership," *Harvard Business Review*, November–December, pp. 68–74.

Haken, H. (1981) *The Science of Structure: Synergetics.* Van Nostrand Reinhold, New York, NY, pp. 19, 236.

Hamson, N. et al. (1997) *After Atlantis: Working, Managing and Leading in Turbulent Times.* Butterworth–Heinemann, Boston, MA, p. 38.

Heckman, F. (1997) "Designing Organizations for New Experiences," *The Journal for Quality and Participation*, March, pp. 24–33.

Kelly, K. (1994) *Out of Control: The Rise of Neo-biological Civilization.* William Patrick Books, Addison-Wesley, New York, NY, p. 2.

Klein, E.H. and Izzo, J.B. (1998) *Awakening Corporate Soul.* Fairwinds Press, New York, NY, p. 107.

Kohn, A. (1992) *No Contest: The Case Against Competition.* Houghton Mifflin, New York, NY, p. 61.

Mascarenhas, B., Baveja, A. and Jamil, M. (1998) "Dynamic Core Competencies in Leading Multinational Companies," *California Management Review*, Vol. 40, No. 4, Summer, pp. 117–132.

Matson, E. (1998) "Job Success Now Hinges on Projects," *The Salt Lake Tribune*, February 8, pp. E1, E5–E6.

Petzinger, T., Jr. (1999) *The New Pioneers.* Simon & Schuster, New York, NY, pp. 27–32.

Pfeffer, T. and Veiga, T.F. (1999) "Putting People First for Organizational Success," *Academy of Management Executives*, Vol. 13, No. 2, May, pp. 37–48.

Prahalad, C.K. and Hamel, G. (1990) "The Core Competence of the Corporation," *Harvard Business Review*, May–June, pp. 79–91.

Wheatley, M.J. (1992) *Leadership and the New Science: Learning About Organization from an Orderly Universe.* Berrett-Koehler, San Francisco, CA, p. 93.

7

Generating, Capturing, and Leveraging Intellectual Capital

Everything becomes a little different as soon as it is spoken out loud.

Hermann Hesse

The purpose of this chapter is to present a comprehensive model depicting the integrated dynamic processes needed for creating highly sustained levels of intellectual assets. Although the model shows how to put theory into practice, it is not a prescriptive framework. Rather, it provides a *general* configuration essential for continuous knowledge generation, with the proviso that every organization will develop its own unique qualities suited for its members and environmental conditions.

This model is different from others either being advocated or currently in use because it clearly shows the vital links between social capital generation, intellectual capital generation, and market responsiveness. For instance, it makes little sense to focus exclusively on intellectual asset creation (which most companies seem to be doing) before developing a solid social capital foundation consisting of something similar to the four tenets for unleashing human nature discussed in Chapter 5. As stated throughout, intellectual capital generation is indispensably tied to the intensity of idea sharing and integration; therefore, knowledge amplification depends on the openness of individuals, teams, and the organization as a whole.

That is, without the *balanced* expression of the self-centered and other-centered innate human drives, a shared-access social system cannot emerge. Consequently, high levels of tacit knowledge sharing are almost impossible to attain, limiting the expansion of explicit knowledge, requisite variety, and the continual upgrading of organizational core competencies. The results are poor market responsiveness, by not developing world-class products and services and not getting them to customers rapidly, and inadequate financial returns to the company and its members. Yet most organizations continue to concentrate primarily on intellectual capital alone.

KNOWLEDGE APPLICATION STRATEGIES

A recently completed study of knowledge application practices involving firms in several industries by Hansen, Nohria, and Tierney (1999) concluded that the methods fall into two general categories: codification and personalization. In the codification category, "knowledge is carefully codified and stored in databases, where it can be accessed and used easily by anyone in the company." Conversely, in firms applying the personalization strategy, "knowledge is closely tied to the person who developed it and is shared mainly through direct person-to-person contacts. The chief purpose of computers at such companies is to help people communicate knowledge, not to store it." Which strategy is employed by an organization "depends on the way the company serves it clients, the economics of the business, and the people it hires." According to the authors, companies such as Andersen Consulting, Ernst & Young, Access Health, and Dell use the codification mode, whereas McKinsey & Company, Bain & Company, Memorial Sloan-Kettering Cancer Center, and Hewlett-Packard employ the personalized strategy.

I consider the codification methodology of knowledge use to be founded on the machine-logic of the Industrial Age. The personalized strategy, on the other hand, is clearly based on bio-logic and self-organizing principles more attuned to the Knowledge Age. For instance, the former strategy relies almost exclusively on the repetitive use of explicit knowledge and people accustomed to the reuse of the same knowledge in implementing standard solutions. The latter methodology, however, depends primarily on tacit knowledge sharing and individuals with high tolerance for ambiguity and abilities to solve unique problems. From an economic standpoint, one strategy depends on generating large overall revenues (high volume sales) and the other on high profit margins from highly customized products and services.

Currently, as we transition from the Industrial Age to the Knowledge Age, either strategy is viable. I suggest, however, that as we leave the Industrial Age farther and farther behind, the personalized strategy of knowledge development and application will increasingly gain dominance. When uncertainty, ambiguity, and strategic discontinuities become the norm, driven by technological change and global hypercompetition, reusable explicit knowledge will become less pertinent. Hence, analytically rigorous skills for situation-specific problem solving dependent on high levels of tacit knowledge will take center stage.

In either case, the comprehensive knowledge generation model described in this chapter can support both strategic options. Discernibly, the model will be of greater value to those organizations that are or are planning to employ customized knowledge to situation-specific problems or opportunities. Undoubtedly, however, companies relying on the codified mode of knowledge management periodically need to update and at times completely change their intellectual capital base; therefore, my models will be helpful even to companies using the reusable knowledge methodology unless they choose to outsource or purchase the advanced intellectual assets they need.

Several key points need to be emphasized as we examine Figure 7.1. First, the model is a dynamic nonequilibrium parallel operating system that does not function in a cause-and-effect or serial sequence. *All* components of the system work together simultaneously similar to any self-organizing entity. Thus, the model is founded on bio-logic instead of machine-logic, and any change taking place in one part of the system will have an immediate effect on the rest of the system. Essentially, the system organizes itself, but no agent coordinates activities from inside the system. Success for knowledge-based organizations depends on some form of self-organization because knowledge

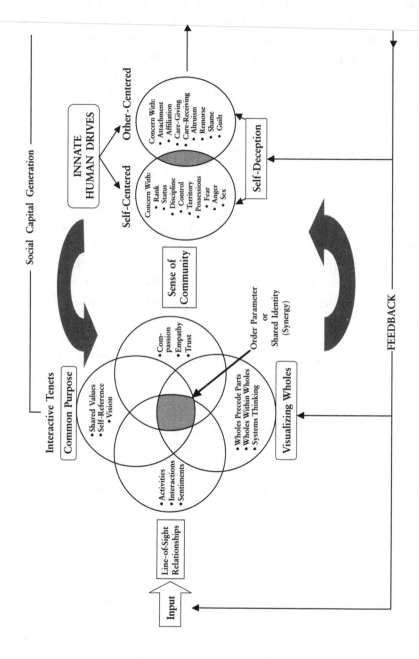

Figure 7.1A   *Generating, Capturing, and Leveraging Intellectual Capital, Part I.*

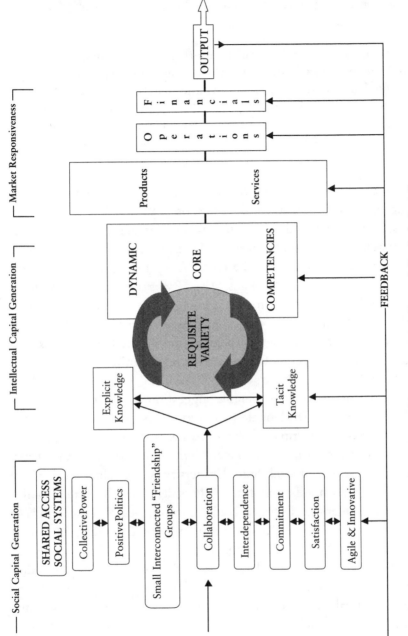

Figure 7.1B Generating, Capturing, and Leveraging Intellectual Capital, Part II.

cannot be managed or collected. As Thomas Petzinger (1999) eloquently stated:

> 'Knowledge management' is another great oxymoron. Al-
> though information can be managed—in spreadsheets,
> books, and databases, for instance—no one can manage
> knowledge. This is not just a subtlety of semantics. Knowing
> about knowledge and respecting it will help prevent compa-
> nies from backsliding into the twenty-first-century equiva-
> lent of Taylorism.

Second, I did not pull the Generating, Capturing, and Leveraging Intellectual Capital Model out of "thin air." In the past ten
years, I have expanded my research from management and organizational behavior into other diverse fields as described in Chapter 1. In
the process, I have heeded the comments of practitioners engaged
daily in running their businesses. Also, I was a manager in both the
public and private sectors for 23 years before becoming immersed in
higher education. More specifically, I have spent the last three years
almost exclusively fleshing out the models presented in this book, and
what I have developed is founded on solid scientific evidence.

Third, several scholars and practitioners reviewed my prelimi-
nary draft and provided invaluable suggestions and comments. These
individuals include Dr. Donald F. Summers, Associate Director of the
National Cancer Institute; John Giovale, a prominent member of
W.L. Gore & Associates; Dr. Peter Gerity, biologist and Vice Presi-
dent for Research at Utah State University; Carl Lehmann, CEO of
RTW in Minneapolis and former President of The Stored Value
Group of American Express; Ned Hamson, Senior Editor of *The
Journal for Quality and Participation*; and noted author and consul-
tant Margaret Wheatley, to name a few.

Finally, if you still need more proof that the model can be widely
applied, let me quote Percy Barnevik, the former CEO of ABB (Joyce,
1992): "I'd rather be roughly right and fast than exactly right and
slow. The cost of delay is greater than the cost of an occasional mis-
take." In the Knowledge Age, hesitating to find and apply *fully tested
ways* to accelerate the expansion of intellectual assets can have irreversible consequences. Further, as mentioned in Chapter 6, Thomas
Petzinger (1999) has provided ample evidence why and how self-

organizing systems are the wave of the future. Also, many of the major components of Figure 7.1 were recently published by *Business Horizons* (Ehin, 1998). However, the best proof of the model's effectiveness is W.L. Gore & Associates as described in Chapter 5. They have used the fundamental principles of the systems for more than 40 years with extraordinary success.

THE SYSTEM'S LIFEBLOOD

The model's vital inputs are information and people. I will focus on information and knowledge later when we get to the intellectual capital generation portion of the model. First, however, the emphasis will be on the selection of people. Who is invited to join the "clan" of no more than approximately 150 individuals will undoubtedly determine the levels of social and intellectual capital that the organization can generate and sustain.

We are all keenly aware of the difficulties that can emerge in any social setting to undermine collaborative efforts. These problems usually include personality clashes, unwillingness to resolve conflicts, struggles over common goals, and strong performers wanting excessive compensation or nonperformers wanting too much credit. Being selective in screening prospective associates or partners does not eliminate these difficulties. Vigorous selection processes do, however, lessen the subsequent frequency and intensity of the clashes that develop, allowing a more supportive environment where voluntary collaboration becomes the mainstay to evolve.

The key factor for successful social capital generation is to ensure that both the self-centered and other-centered innate human drives have an opportunity to be expressed in a balanced fashion. In order for that delicate balance to occur, constituents of the organization must believe that they are indeed working with close friends who can be relied on and trusted. Therefore, during the selection process, organizational members are literally searching for new "family" members with whom they can work closely and socialize on and off the job.

Essentially, the overall emphasis must be on developing and maintaining a small clan-size shared-access operation whose activities revolve exclusively around a limited number of *world-class* capabilities. Hence, peripheral functions and skills that are needed to support the organization's core competencies, but that do not provide a competitive advantage, are best outsourced or performed by joint venture partners who are proficient in those undertakings. Consequently, the selection process needs to concentrate on finding and attracting individuals whose knowledge, skills, experiences, intuition, and values can further enhance the dynamic core capabilities of the company. For instance, the core competencies at Hewlett-Packard revolve around communications, computation, and measurement, and a high priority is placed on values that support tacit knowledge sharing.

Obviously, the people who join a firm that either is or wishes to function in a shared-access mode must have the necessary knowledge and skills to add value to its core competencies. More important, however, they also need to be competent, self-reliant, and motivated individuals who are willing to become responsible associates or partners. That is, they must be able to work both independently and in teams and prepared to assume responsibility and accountability for the activities of the entire organization. The ultimate purpose is to seek a good fit and buy-in of the individual.

In order to satisfy these stringent requirements, the recruiting process should use a multifaceted approach, but even that will not guarantee success. Not only is organizational fit hard to determine, but people also currently change jobs an average of every four years. Finding and retaining competent people is especially important in knowledge-intensive companies. Without extended periods of association and collaboration, high levels of social and intellectual capital are almost impossible to maintain. Therefore, well-suited individuals should be invited to become partners in the endeavor, not employees. Employees are "mercenaries" easily enticed by the highest bidders. Partners, on the other hand, are investors and part owners whose welfare depends on the continuous success of the entire enterprise. Partnerships also limit the size of an organization to approximately 150 people.

Selection of partners should include testing and extensive multiday interviews. I recommend using at least two test instruments in the recruitment proceedings. To begin with, a five-factor model, referred to as the "Big 5," has emerged in the past 10 to 15 years through extensive research. This model can profile an individual's personality structure with a high degree of accuracy. The five dimensions of the model include extroversion-introversion, agreeableness, openness to experience, conscientiousness, and emotional stability. Unquestionably, all five factors are important indicators for success in a shared-access context. More important, studies show that conscientiousness and extroversion are positively correlated with exceptional job performance when the job has a high degree of autonomy.

Wonderlic, Inc., in Libertyville, Illinois, has a reliable test instrument for the Big 5 called the Personal Characteristics Inventory developed by Dr. Murray Barrick and Michael Mount of the University of Iowa. Wonderlic also has a test that profiles an individual's entrepreneurial tendencies. I recommend the optional use of the entrepreneurial instrument.

The other test I suggest using in the selection process is the Myers-Briggs Type Indicator. This test measures the dimensions of extroversion-introversion, sensing-intuiting, thinking-feeling, and judging-perceiving. Extroverts get their energy from interacting with other people, whereas introverts recharge in solitude. Sensing people want facts, trust facts, and believe in facts; intuiting people are imaginative, intellectually playful, and innovative. Thinking types are comfortable with impersonal, objective, rational decisions; feeling types are comfortable with personal decisions that flow from value positions. Finally, judging types prefer closure, whereas perceiving types prefer options. I favor the use of the Keirsey Temperament Sorter (Keirsey, 1998), which is a short variation of the Myers-Briggs Type Indicator. It consists of only 70 questions, can be taken in approximately 15 minutes, and is easily self-scored. It can also be found on the Internet.

Similar to all survey instruments, these tests provide only general indications of personality types and an approximation of how people think. They should not be used as the primary means to screen people. They are best used to assure that an organization has a good mix of different categories of individuals who are competent self-starters willing and able to closely interact with others. That is, you want to develop a cohesive network of people who also welcome constructive conflict in an atmosphere of trust when critically analyzing ideas.

The mainstay of the selection process is the personal interview. Although also imperfect, it provides the best means of accomplishing two vital functions: One is to allow as many members of the organization as possible face-to-face contact with a candidate in order to provide a good "feel" for the "clan fit" of the person. The other is to provide the applicant with ample opportunity to determine if he or she wants to join the clan. Interviews should be multi-day affairs, giving the candidate and the company's associates a reasonable chance to determine if the fit is indeed mutually acceptable.

SOCIAL CAPITAL GENERATION

Having examined the lifeblood of the model, we should now be ready to put the system into motion. The *only* people who can have the true desire and the detailed organizational knowledge and skills to breathe life into the comprehensive intellectual capital generation system I am advocating are those individuals who have a stake in its success—the citizens of the mini-community or the company. Who else knows better what has to be accomplished and why certain functions are more important than others?

I champion the fundamental philosophy of "participative design," developed by Fred and Merrelyn Emery (Hamson et al., 1997) and discussed in the previous chapter, for implementing enduring change. Therefore, after a two- or three-day seminar on the details of the intellectual capital generation model attended by all clan members, attendees should be "let loose" to begin designing their own *unique* system appropriate for their circumstances.

No "cookie cutter" methodology can be used to generate intellectual assets. The people involved, not some experts or an experimental group, should be responsible for the system from beginning to end. They determine where and how to start, when and whom to ask for assistance, and what and when training is needed. In essence, the owners (partners) determine what their house should look like, what comforts it will have, and who will live in it. Thus, "as the number of connections between people and things add up, the consequences of those connections multiply out even faster, so that initial successes aren't self-limiting, but self-feeding" (Kelly, 1998).

Social capital generation begins with the four tenets for foster-ing human nature and ends with an established interdependent shared-access context. The tenets are the wellsprings for unleashing the duality of innate human drives in a balanced manner. Recall Fig-ure 4.1; essentially, the goal is to move away from the controlled-access context, which depends primarily on the activities of the two lower levels of the brain, to the shared-access mode, where the neo-cortex has as much free range as possible to spawn new ideas. As suggested in Chapter 5, the tenets are social competencies that must be cultivated into existence and that are grounded in emergent be-havior. Also, the social system cannot function effectively in the shared-access mode if one of the tenets is either missing or has not been fully developed.

Without repeating too much of what has already been discussed, I will suggest what needs to be accomplished in developing the four tenets and how members of an organization know when they have sufficient social capital. This goal can best be accomplished by asking a lot of detailed questions that the associates can mostly answer them-selves. Again, this process places responsibility for the organization development effort squarely on the shoulders of the constituents and not on some "guru." It is all about self-help, not about following in-structions to the letter. It is also about sharing tacit knowledge.

First, line-of-sight relationships are best achieved through truly voluntary teams. That is, people should be able to join and leave teams as they see fit, and they should also have an opportunity to be part of more than one team. For that process to take place effectively, associates need a certain amount of training in social-emotional skills, task skills, and team skills. For example, people need to know how to be supportive, how to express their feelings without being antagonis-tic, how to be assertive in a positive way, and how to listen for con-tent and feelings. They should also comprehend how best to solve problems, make decisions, set goals, critique, and plan in a team set-ting. These skills require some expert help. Without it, individual psy-chological empowerment and sustained mutually beneficial intellec-tual growth are difficult to attain.

With some help from Ruth Wageman's (1997) excellent article, "Critical Success Factors for Creating Superb Self-Managing Teams," I have compiled the following list of questions that organizational members can use to see how far they have progressed and what areas need further attention concerning line-of-sight relationships:

1. Is team membership completely voluntary?
2. Is a general guideline used regarding how many teams an individual can be a member of at one time?
3. How much time is devoted for initial and recurring team development training? Interteam training?
4. Are adequate numbers of trained facilitators available to any team as the situation requires?
5. Can all team members articulate clear direction of their work and specific goals? Do the *self-imposed* goals stretch their performance? Have specific timelines been agreed to when the goals are to be completed? Have specific interrelationships with other internal or external individuals/teams been clearly defined?
6. Are individual, team, and organizational goals and the progress toward those goals posted for *everyone* to be able to monitor and relate their performance to those goals?
7. Are individual and team rewards directly related to value-added activities?
8. Do the teams have the authority and responsibility to decide the following:
   - When and how to meet customer demands
   - What action to take
   - How to change work strategies when deemed necessary
9. Do team members:
   - Encourage each other to detect problems on their own?
   - Openly discuss differences in what everyone needs to contribute to the team?
   - Encourage each other to experiment with new processes/ methods?
   - Constantly seek to learn from other teams?
10. Is everyone in teams cross-trained in order to help each other?
11. Can team members clearly articulate the interdependence and mutual benefits derived from intra- and inter-team work?
12. Do team members feel they are able to largely "mind read" or anticipate the behavior/actions of others in forging bonds of trust and developing/completing projects?

Next, a true sense of community is physiologically impossible to attain with membership exceeding 150 people, as stipulated previously. Also, partnerships become too diluted and meaningless beyond that limit. However, that does not mean large enterprises cannot make use of the model. Similar to W.L. Gore & Associates or ABB, they can organize into clan-size independent units connected to each other by a superordinate vision and the sharing of ideas and resources for competitive advantage. Thus, an organization can benefit from being both large and small simultaneously.

Fundamentally, a sense of community is determined by the patterns of connections between its members; the respect and friendships that develop through those connections; and the shared representations, interpretations, and systems of meanings that evolve. In Chapter 3, I mentioned that the central focus of the higher brain functions is perceptual categorization, which allows people to match their behavior to the demands of their immediate environment. A sense of community has a tremendous impact on our social and intellectual well being. An atmosphere of a community can be best achieved through the interaction of multiple voluntary teams whose members serve on more than one team. Hence, the organization also requires a certain amount of inter-team training and development. The following list of questions gives an indication of the depth of community relationships:

1. Do clan members feel safe from negative politics, power struggles, and personal threats?
2. Does the organizational environment support free expression of values and beliefs?
3. Does the work context support making voluntary meaningful contributions that benefit the entire organization?
4. Are new perspectives and ideas encouraged and welcomed?
5. Does everyone have an overall strong sense of belonging, compassion, empathy, and trust of other clan members?
6. Do people feel responsible and accountable not only for the success of their own team(s) but also other teams within the clan?
7. Do members share the need to distribute rewards equitably in good times and bad times based on their value-added activities?

8. Does the clan support and have provisions to incubate and spin off new products or services?

Common purpose, the third tenet, is about finding worthwhile strategies for *mutual* survival. It helps organizational members to take a balanced approach between concern for self and concern for others. To achieve that end requires a strong sense of partnership. The level of common purpose achieved or needing to be achieved can generally be determined by the ensuing questions:

1. Do organizational members consider themselves to be partners or employees?
2. Do all members:
   - Have the right to say no?
   - Feel they have joint accountability?
   - Base their activities on honesty and mutual trust?
   - Share relatively common values and beliefs?
3. Do people have an accurate understanding of the current state of affairs, including who their customers are and the strengths of their competitors?
4. Does a compelling shared vision exist based on the answers to the following three questions:
   - Are my key personal survival needs best satisfied by being or becoming a member of this social institution? (individual-level question)
   - What do we want to accomplish together? (clan-level question)
   - Who are we trying to serve? (clan-level question)

The final tenet, visualizing wholes, is the conceptual categorization that provides organizational members with an appreciation of the interconnectedness among themselves and their external constituencies. It starts with individual perceptions and then spreads throughout the organization. The focus is on relationships, processes, and integration instead of on individual parts, functions, or tasks. Visualizing wholes should also include a systems view of life in general to better understand relationships with others, ourselves, and our constant process of transformation. Three broad questions help to discover the prevalence or absence of systems thinking:

1. Do members perceive themselves to be vital partners within the organization and its extended external constituencies?
2. Is every individual and team able to visualize the impact of their activities or intended activities on other members, teams, and the processes of the entire organization?
3. Does every member and team understand the importance of having and maintaining informal and formal links with external networks and agencies?

The order parameter or shared identity is the most essential, yet the most ambiguous, part of the social capital generation portion of the model because it deals more with a feeling than with something concrete and visible. Winning teams, for instance, have that feeling. Inherently, the order parameter is the building and propelling force emanating from the interplay of the four tenets, which must be fully developed to support the process.

A shared identity is an emergent property that is created by the voluntary cooperation of autonomous members of a system who constantly experiment with new mutually beneficial positions and re-action processes. The order parameter can best be compared to the improvisation abilities of a good jazz band when they are in "the groove." The shared identity cannot be copied by other groups, which gives those that have attained it a competitive advantage. The following three questions may provide clues to the existence of a shared identity:

1. Does coordination without control exist among organizational members and teams?
2. Is there form (a sense of unity) without an imposed organizational structure?
3. Is there a sense of an "invisible hand" moving the clan toward a shared vision without restricting the freedom of its autonomous members and teams?

The central factors of the social capital generation process are the innate human drives. Without understanding their physiological significance, it is impossible to grasp the difference between machine-logic and bio-logic and the need to abandon the Industrial Age paradigms of resource management. Maintaining organizational contexts where primarily the self-centered drives are expressed cannot be changed to be more participative by slogans and pep rallies. Such catch phrases only increase cynicism and are counterproductive for broadening an organization's knowledge base. The goal must be to unleash human nature and its inherent intelligence in a balanced fashion and to not hold it back by catering to our more primitive side.

As described in detail in Chapter 3, innate drives are certain human predisposed and genetically determined behavior patterns expressed in response to specific environmental conditions. They differ from our instincts because we have a choice about how we act out these predispositions. People function best when both the self-centered and other-centered drives have an opportunity to be expressed in a balanced manner so that neither side dominates, as the shaded area in Figure 7.1 depicts. To get a better "feel" for which side of the innate drives is being expressed more than the other, organizational members can complete and score the following short sample survey. The survey should be followed up with focus groups and interviews. If the self-centered side dominates, then more work needs to be done in developing the four tenets.

How much are you concerned with (circle the applicability of each item on a scale from 1 to 10, with 10 being the most applicable response):

Rank	1	2	3	4	5	6	7	8	9	10
Status	1	2	3	4	5	6	7	8	9	10
Discipline	1	2	3	4	5	6	7	8	9	10
Control	1	2	3	4	5	6	7	8	9	10
Territory	1	2	3	4	5	6	7	8	9	10
Possessions	1	2	3	4	5	6	7	8	9	10
Fear	1	2	3	4	5	6	7	8	9	10
Anger	1	2	3	4	5	6	7	8	9	10

How much are you concerned with (circle the applicability of each item on a scale from 1 to 10, with 10 being the most applicable response):

Attachment	1	2	3	4	5	6	7	8	9	10
Affiliation	1	2	3	4	5	6	7	8	9	10
Care giving	1	2	3	4	5	6	7	8	9	10

Care receiving	1	2	3	4	5	6	7	8	9	10
Altruism	1	2	3	4	5	6	7	8	9	10
Shame	1	2	3	4	5	6	7	8	9	10
Guilt	1	2	3	4	5	6	7	8	9	10

As the model delineates, with the large curved arrows rotating from the interactive tenets to the innate drives and back to the tenets, continuous circular causality takes place between these two elements of the system; the process is self-perpetuating. That is, constant reinforcement of the drives in a balanced manner affects physical changes in the synapses of the brain as specific neural pathways are emphasized. The circular causality that develops as a result further positively reinforces the development of the tenets, which, in turn, reinforce the appropriate innate drives, and so on.

The result of this dynamic process between the interactive tenets and the equalized innate drives is the emergence of a shared-access social system critical for supporting voluntary collaboration and sharing of tacit knowledge. Inherently, the shared-access social construct is an overt self-organizing system whose members share equitably the responsibility and accountability for the management of all organizational resources. To determine which context (controlled-access or shared-access) prevails in a firm, use Boxes 4.1 and 4.2.

INTELLECTUAL CAPITAL GENERATION

The tightly coupled dynamic components constituting the intellectual capital generation portion of the model are explicit knowledge, tacit knowledge, requisite variety, and dynamic core competencies. Again, these components, like the entire model, are parallel operating systems that work together simultaneously. The parts can only be separated for analysis purposes.

The explicit knowledge element is probably the simplest to explain, although that does not mean it is the least important part of the system. As discussed in Chapter 5, explicit knowledge has been codified into documents, databases, articles, books, lectures, and so on. Whoever can gain access to it can interpret it and use it. A good example of accessibility to explicit knowledge is the use of the Internet. Obviously, it can be easily transmitted (once found) and used by anyone who finds it useful. Explicit knowledge, therefore, does not provide much competitive leverage unless it is a closely guarded trade secret or a patent.

Although explicit knowledge does not provide competitive leverage, organization members still must keep abreast of explicit knowledge generated both internally and by suppliers, competitors (including potential competitors), and customers. Such knowledge needs to be constantly collected, classified, and stored so it is easily accessible to all associates of the firm. Therefore, an organization must make reasonable investments in information technology and the maintenance of these systems. As suggested by Kevin Kelly (1998), in an age where innovation is continuously accelerating and when "the soft trumps the hard, the most powerful technologies are those that enhance, amplify, extend, augment, distill, recall, expand, and develop soft relationships of all types." But the use of information technology alone, no matter how sophisticated, will not be enough. An organization also needs to have a strong information-sharing culture, which is why social capital is such a vital part of the model.

The following list of explicit knowledge sources should be placed in specially designed repositories that are easily accessible to all members of a knowledge-intensive company:

- Individual and team skills/knowledge files
- Organizational expertise:
    1. Unique technological capabilities
    2. Distinctive process or coordination skills
    3. Special abilities for establishing external relationships
- Completed project files showing what was planned, what actually transpired, why there was a difference and the lessons learned
- Internal publications
- External publications
- Selected links to external databases
- Formal training opportunities and schedules
- Formal information provided by suppliers and customers
- Links to professional organizations

- Competitor and potential competitor files
- Organizational reputation compiled from various internal and external sources

Tacit or unrelated knowledge is a much more indeterminate subject than explicit knowledge. As examined previously, tacit knowledge is acquired through first-hand experiences or by working with more knowledgeable people. It encompasses ideas and abstractions at the individual level. As opposed to explicit knowledge, tacit knowledge cannot be found in documents, databases, books, or files. It can only be shared orally and, therefore, it cannot be transmitted.

Thus, tacit knowledge is part of a never-ending cycle between it and explicit knowledge. That is, as tacit knowledge is formalized, captured, and leveraged through person-to-person interactions, it becomes explicit. Subsequently, explicit knowledge triggers more tacit knowledge ad infinitum. Tacit knowledge must be allowed to emerge through self-organization; it cannot be forced out of people or copied. Tacit knowledge is the ultimate source of competitive advantage. The following processes (among others) can support tacit knowledge generation and sharing:

- Projects in progress
- Experimentation
- Periodic reflection
- Frequent socialization
- Developing and maintaining informal external networks and relationships with other experts, customers, suppliers, government agencies, etc.

Finally, formalizing, capturing, and leveraging tacit knowledge needs to take place at three levels: individual, team, and the organization as a whole.

Individual level. Each member of the organization needs to be constantly encouraged to do the following:
   1. Develop and maintain informal internal and external relationships with other experts, customers, suppliers, and other entities for sharing of ideas.

2. Experiment on their own with new ideas, methods, and concepts by writing papers, presenting papers, and attending professional conferences.
3. Socialize as often as possible with people who are experts in similar or related fields. However, don't ignore people who "seem" to be engaged in totally unrelated areas because these contacts often trigger serendipitous ideas that are impossible to predict or anticipate.
4. Ravenously read professional journals in both related and unrelated fields.
5. Think about "things" that seem currently impossible to do but that would be beneficial if a way to accomplish them could be found.

Team level. Each team should:
1. Develop close bonds within a team and with other teams within the clan.
2. Socialize off the job often.
3. Set time aside for reflection on projects in progress and to experiment or brainstorm with new ideas, concepts, and processes.
4. Develop and maintain informal networks external to the clan.

Clan level. The organization as a whole should:
1. Have frequent meetings where individuals and teams can share their experiments and new ideas, concepts, and processes with all clan members.
2. Sponsor frequent social events where everyone has an opportunity to maintain relationships with other individuals whom they are not in constant contact with on a day-to-day basis.
3. Do everything possible to develop and maintain an atmosphere within the clan that helps everyone to sense that "we are all in this together no matter what."
4. Maintain an easy-to-use system that allows new ideas, no matter how vaguely defined, to be posted and accessible to all clan members.

Similar to the order parameter or shared identity in the social capital generation portion of the model, requisite variety is the central component of the intellectual capital production side. The law of requisite variety, as reviewed in Chapter 6, stipulates that for a system to properly survive, it must be capable of matching whatever complexity its environment presents. Thus, without proper requisite variety, an organization is "driving blind." Requisite variety depends on constant sharing of information and ideas with organizational members and external networks and effective environmental scanning. It is generated by the dynamic interplay of explicit knowledge, tacit knowledge, and core competencies of the system. Requisite variety essentially provides high-velocity responsiveness for the organization.

Maintaining proper levels of internal and external awareness are the key factors for effective requisite variety propagation. The following outline can be used to gauge internal and external awareness:

Internal Awareness. How familiar are organizational members and teams of the following:
- Skills/knowledge of individuals and teams within the clan
- Overall organizational expertise in the following areas: select technologies, specific processes, or relationships with external agencies/networks
- Projects completed by the organization
- Papers/proposals written by clan members or teams
- Information available from suppliers and customers
- Clan memberships in professional organizations
- Specific training/education available internally
- Overall reputation of the organization compared to competitors and the specific basis for that reputation

External Awareness. How familiar are organizational members and teams of the following:
- Skills/knowledge of competitors or potential competitors around the world
- Skills/knowledge of current suppliers and potential suppliers
- Domestic and global industry trends
- Technologic and process trends/projections worldwide

- Domestic and global demographic, fashion, and lifestyle trends
- Worldwide environmental projections
- Anticipated impact of the trends/projections on the core competencies of the organization
- Organizational links with various networks and agencies and the impact of those relationships to the core competencies

Probably one of the best ways for a company to attain and sustain suitable levels of requisite variety in the Knowledge Age is to follow the "Mission Statement for the Learning Organization" developed by the Center for Managerial Learning and Simulation at Georgia Southern University headed by Bernard Keys (Fulmer, Gibbs, and Keys, 1998). It reads as follows:

> The world changes and we cannot stop it. Our products will change, our markets will change, our customers will change, and some of our employees will move on—we hope to greater things. But these things will not change—we will learn faster than our competitors; we will learn across our organization from each other and from teams; we will learn externally from our suppliers and our customers; we will learn vertically from top to bottom of our organization; we will ask the right questions and use action learning; we will anticipate the future and create scenarios to learn from it; we will practice what we learn and learn from practice; we will learn faster than our environment changes; we will learn where no man or woman has learned before; therefore, we will survive and prosper.

Dynamic core competencies—a unique set of resources that arise from collective organizational learning to give a firm its competitive advantage—emerge from intellectual capital generation. They are difficult-to-coordinate discrete production or service skills that integrate varied streams of people and technologies. They provide access to a wide range of markets and are extremely hard to imitate by competitors because of their uniqueness. Innovative products and services are the by-products of dynamic core competencies. Obviously, these competencies cannot remain static or they would turn into core rigidities, which would lead to certain organizational decline.

As stipulated previously, core competencies can be categorized into three broad areas of collective learning: expertise in certain technologies, coordination or process skills, and abilities in developing and maintaining external relationships or networks (Mascarenhas, Baveja, and Jamil, 1998). Therefore, if an organization is to maintain its competitive edge, every one of its constituents should be able to articulate the following:

1. Identify the core competencies (usually no more than approximately six) of the organization and how they are used to develop/produce leading-edge products and services.
2. Describe how the core competencies are constantly nurtured and updated.
3. Explain how the core competencies provide access to a wide variety of markets, make significant contributions to customer benefits, and are difficult to imitate by competitors.

MARKET RESPONSIVENESS

The final component of the model is straightforward other than for the financials portion. If the social and intellectual capital parts of the system are in sync, then producing a constant stream of innovative and market-responsive products or services should not be difficult. These products or services most likely will also have superior price and performance attributes.

The operations part of the system includes the standard elements of a business value chain. That is, for the firm to stay viable, it must be able to market and sell its products or services. Production, logistics, and after-sales services must also be included. Last but not least, human resource management functions need to be performed to ensure that the organization at least complies with state and federal laws. As previously suggested, these functions can be outsourced or performed by joint venture partners. The organization should avoid doing anything where it does not have a world-class competitive advantage.

The financials portion of the model also includes mostly standard operating requirements such as profit and loss statements and other legally required documentation. Financial plans for internal use as well should be the purview of this function. Most important, however, the financial process should be able to provide each organizational member and team with direct and up-to-date information on their contributions or value-adding activities. That is, disbursement of income and profits to associates should be directly linked to individual and team output. We must remember that we are dealing with partners, not employees. Therefore, everyone benefits in accordance with their contributions to the organization's success.

If the total system is configured properly, its output should provide customers with continuous high levels of satisfaction and success. In addition, the organization should be able to maintain or increase its market responsiveness, profit margins, and reputation. Finally, the system should also afford its members personal contentment and equitable benefits.

I have presented a comprehensive model for generating, capturing, and leveraging intellectual capital. I hope I have succeeded in demonstrating how intellectual capital creation is indispensably tied to idea sharing and integration, and, as a result, why focusing exclusively on knowledge expansion before developing a firm social foundation is illogical. Without the balanced expression of innate human drives, high levels of tacit knowledge sharing are almost impossible to attain, forcing the organization to rely primarily on available explicit knowledge. Such an approach provides a firm with little competitive advantage in the Knowledge Age.

AN EXAMPLE

After reading a draft of this chapter, Carl Champagne, the President and CEO of Data Systems International, informed me that it reminded him of another case from his past. What was most surprising to both of us, was that without knowing or using the terminology of Figure 7.1, he had used many of the components of the model to turn around a floundering company more than a decade ago. Here again is Champagne explaining the situation.

In the late 1980s, I had the opportunity to lead a firm that employed approximately 150 people in manufacturing essential equipment for television stations. The organization I headed was part of a group of stand-alone enterprises of a large publicly traded corporation providing products to the broadcast video market segment of the industry. It was also the group's largest revenue producer and its most profitable business at the time.

Ironically, the company had gone through three presidents in four years prior to my arrival. What was even more intriguing was the fact that the presidents of the other firms reporting to the group vice president had experienced the same fate. Why? Primarily because these executives had been unable to accurately forecast revenue and profit margins for their respective organizations. The culprit turned out to be the group vice president, who insisted on receiving faultless predictions while simultaneously providing little autonomy to the presidents to run their firms. The situation was classic micromanagement at its best.

Needless to say, things were in relative disarray when I took over the company. Morale was low, development of new products was almost at a standstill, and little interaction occurred among departments. The environment was not conducive to "intellectual capital generation." I knew immediately that it was not going to be easy turning this business around. Fortunately, I had insisted on being given full rein in making any changes I deemed necessary before I accepted the position. I was reluctantly given that autonomy, as long as I could forecast higher returns and make or exceed those predictions.

Obviously, time was of the essence because I had to show positive results quickly. Thus, I brought with me a seasoned executive team consisting of people with whom I had previously worked. This preformed team lessened the time I needed to establish the necessary relationships with organizational members. In terms of Professor Ehin's model, part of the "social capital" required to revitalize the company came with the senior staff. What amazes me looking back is that our initial effort was focused on developing an effective social system using something like the Four Tenets for Fostering Human Nature.

First, we reviewed and became acquainted with the existing systems and processes. Problems, issues, and recommendations to alleviate these concerns were then solicited from all corners of the organization. Next, a vision, mission, and shared values were defined for the company with the involvement of all its members. That process was followed by forming self-managing teams around specific core technologies. Information systems were refined or put in place to provide every team with real-time feedback on orders, bookings, revenues, gross margins, expenses, and profitability. With this information, all teams were able to gauge their own performance and effectiveness. Finally, extensive training programs were established for team development and upgrading of technical skills. Essentially, the purpose of the training was to attain and maintain high levels of social capital.

At first, most people were not convinced that the changes taking place were "real" and permanent. The senior staff, however, set the example as organizational members watched very carefully. The command-and-control systems had disappeared. Decisions were being made through dialogue and consensus instead of direct orders and strict operating procedures. Soon it became apparent to everyone that the work context had transformed. It was now not only "safe" but also expected that individuals and teams establish their own goals and determine how best to accomplish them based on overall company objectives. Individuals who could not cope with this new self-organizing or "shared-access" environment left the organization in a short time.

Consequently, team initiatives and productivity went through the roof. New products were developed and existing ones improved. Score cards and progress measurements for each project, as well as their relationships to other programs and the organization as a whole, were displayed on walls all over the plant easily observable for anyone interested. Hence, in accordance with Figure 7.1, tacit knowledge (a term not familiar to me at the time) was continuously made explicit through close collaborative relationships within and among teams. That knowledge, in turn, was used to ensure that the core competencies remained dynamic. As a result, the firm had the requisite variety to effectively respond and prosper in the constantly changing broadcast industry environment.

Wishful thinking? Far from it considering the actual results. The company grew by more than 35 percent from quarter to quarter in an industry with an average growth rate of 12 percent. The organization set the pace in the corporate group for productivity, profitability, and predictability. It generated more than 30 million dollars in revenue in the first year alone. The workforce had also been reduced to 100 people through attrition. Fundamentally, we had created a dynamic self-reinforcing system capable of generating, capturing, and leveraging highly sustained levels of intellectual capital.

Unfortunately, the story has a disappointing ending. In the beginning of my third year as president, I decided to move on after having fulfilled my goals and obligations. Within months after my departure, the leadership of the corporate group opted to amalgamate as many functions as possible. Marketing and sales were combined and manufacturing was consolidated where possible. In less than three years the division began to lose money, and within five years the division with its consolidated businesses was divested.

Looking at Ehin's model, a number of basic principles pertaining to human nature were violated. Groups and teams were consolidated into departments of more than 200 people. These departments were operated in a command-and-control or "controlled-access" mode—do it our way or hit the highway. Feedback from the market went to a few select people. The joy of using individual tacit knowledge was crushed, as was the synergy among and between teams. The failure was yet another cruel lesson in the use of machine-logic instead of bio-logic. Organizations, indeed, need to learn how to leverage our inherent genetic tendencies for competitive advantage to avoid stumbling around blindly and hoping for the best.

KEY CONSIDERATIONS

- It makes little sense to focus on intellectual asset creation before developing a solid social capital foundation consisting of something similar to the four tenets for unleashing human nature discussed in Chapter 5. Inherently, knowledge amplification depends on the openness of individuals, teams, and the organization as a whole. Thus, without the *balanced* expression of the self-centered and other-centered innate human drives, a shared-access social system cannot emerge. Consequently, high levels of tacit knowledge sharing are almost impossible to attain, limiting the expansion of explicit knowledge, requisite variety, and the continual upgrading of organizational core competencies.

- The lifeblood of a knowledge-intensive organization is competent, dedicated people. We are all keenly aware of the difficulties that can emerge in any social setting to undermine collaborative efforts. Being selective in screening prospective associates or partners does not eliminate these difficulties. A vigorous selection process will, however, lessen the subsequent frequency and intensity of the clashes that develop, allowing a more supportive work environment where voluntary collaboration becomes the mainstay to evolve. Therefore, during the selection process, clan members need to literally search for new "family" members with whom they can work closely and socialize on and off the job. Such individuals also need to possess the knowledge, skills, experience, intuition, and values that can further enhance the company's dynamic core competencies. In addition, they must be able to work both independently and in teams and be prepared to assume responsibility and accountability for the activities of the entire organization. The ultimate purpose is to seek fit and buy-in of the individual.

- The *only* people who can have the true desire and the detailed organizational knowledge and skills to breathe life into the comprehensive intellectual capital generation system are those individuals who have a stake in its success. Those are the citizens of the mini-community or members of the company. Who else knows better what has to be accomplished and why certain functions are more important than others? Therefore, after a two- or three-day seminar on the details of the model attended by all associates of the clan, attendees should be "let loose" to begin designing their own *unique* system appropriate for *their* circumstances. No "cookie cutter" methodology can be used to generate intellectual assets. The people involved, not some experts or an experimental group, should be responsible for the system from beginning to end. They will determine where and how to start, when and whom to ask for assistance, and what and where training is needed.

REFERENCES

Ehin, C. (1998) "Fostering Both Sides of Human Nature—The Foundation for Collaborative Relationships," *Business Horizons*, May–June, pp. 15–25.

Fulmer, R.M., Gibbs, P. and Keys, J.B. (1998) "The Second Generation Learning Organization: New Tools for Sustaining Competitive Advantage," *Organizational Dynamics*, Autumn, pp. 7–20.

Hamson, N. et al. (1997) *After Atlantis: Working, Managing and Leading in Turbulent Times*. Butterworth–Heinemann, Boston, MA, p. 38.

Hansen, T.M., Nohria, N. and Tierney, T. (1999) "What's Your Strategy for Managing Knowledge," *Harvard Business Review*, March–April, pp. 106–116.

Joyce, R. (1992) "Global Hero," *International Management*, September, pp. 82–85.

Keirsey, D. (1998) *Please Understand Me II*. Prometheus Nemesis Books, DelMar, CA, pp. 1–13.

Kelly, K. (1998) *New Rules for the New Economy*. Viking, New York, NY, p. 161.

Mascarenhas, B., Baveja, A. and Jamil, M. (1998) "Dynamics of Core Competencies in Leading Multinational Companies," *California Management Review*, Vol. 40, No. 4, Summer, pp. 117–132.

Petzinger, T., Jr. (1999) *The New Pioneers*. Simon & Schuster, New York, NY, p. 151.

Wageman, R. (1997) "Critical Success Factors for Creating Superb Self-Managing Teams," *Organizational Dynamics*, Summer, pp. 49–61.

8

No Longer Slaves of Our Own Making

Each of us is given a pocketful of time to spend
however we may. We use what we will. We waste
what we will. But we can never get back a day.

Roger Wilcox

In the past ten thousand years or so, and especially in the past three hundred years, we have deliberately chosen to design our social institutions with almost one single purpose in mind—to control the behavior of people within them. Consequently, we have unknowingly catered mostly to the whims of our ancient reptilian brain and, in the process, have benefited little from the other 80 percent of our gray matter—the neocortex—from a general societal perspective other than by the contributions of a select few. Each individual and group has an *inherent* biologically derived potential for creativity and innovation. This potential is unique, unlimited, and unpredictable. One can only imagine the possibilities. Both sides of human nature must be allowed expression, however, for this potential to emerge. Once we fully grasp this fundamental principle, we no longer need to be slaves of our own making.

Now that knowledge "management" is the hottest subject since total quality management and reengineering, we need to realize that intellectual capital generation cannot be managed in the traditional manner to which we have become accustomed. Thus, success in the

Knowledge Age demands that we have the foresight to let go of the top-down, command-and-control framework and to embrace the logic of the biological world based on the principles of self-organization or unmanagement. We need to cultivate work environments where our creative predispositions can be unleashed instead of being "regulated" and suppressed.

In this book, I have introduced a choice in the way we manage the resources of our organizations, especially knowledge organizations. By understanding human nature and how it is expressed in response to certain environmental contexts, we can define and differentiate the best possible options. This understanding will help us to develop the voluntary collaborative frameworks within organizations required for the creation and application of intellectual capital in the Knowledge Age. Our options for managing our vital resources have been presented as two diametrically opposed modes of operation. That is, we can either select the controlled-access or hierarchical organizational context, or we can follow our evolutionary path and rediscover the much more strategically sound shared-access mode, or a self-organizing way of life.

I believe that no other basic strategies are available to consider; the scenario is all or nothing. After all, a flat hierarchy is still a hierarchy and, although to a lesser degree, such a structure will predominantly promote self-centered tendencies over other-centered responses. We must understand the framework that evolves from the resource management alternatives, which affect the emergent behavior of the individuals within that context. Genes and the innate drives they encode are activated in response to the environment. Therefore, the two alternatives cannot be taken lightly because they directly affect the organizational configuration, behavior, learning, and ultimately the health of the system as a whole.

If we seek a centralized hierarchical mode, then we must understand the consequences of this selection. An atmosphere of compliance, competitive power, negative politics, domination, and dependence arises when one or a few people control the resources. The levels of authority that are established force those within the system to predominantly express self-centered tendencies such as greed, fear, intimidation, and deceit as they position themselves for greater authority and power. These actions will not necessarily follow the goals of the organization as individuals informally self-organize based on their own best interest. Such a context obviously does not foster knowledge sharing and intellectual capital generation.

Existence within the controlled-access environment is also self-perpetuating. Constant reinforcement of self-centered drives affects physical changes in the synapses of the brain as specific neuronal pathways are emphasized. The circular causality that develops as a result reinforces the controlled-access structure, which, in turn, reinforces self-centered tendencies and so on. As such, slogans, signs, and mottos will not correct the situation. As stated before, we essentially become slaves of our own making.

Is control and compliance what we really want, and is it the best survival strategy, especially for a knowledge-driven society? I think not! I am convinced that sustainable competitive advantage can only be attained through voluntary collaboration that amplifies creativity and innovation by allowing tacit knowledge to emerge and become explicit. Such interactions produce a continuous flow of new, mutually beneficial positions and reaction processes that cannot be easily duplicated by competitors.

Genuine collaboration requires high levels of trust, compassion, and empathy among individuals and teams. Without a sense of community, mutually supportive relationships cannot develop and the inherent intellectual potential of people involved remains dormant. We must remember that other-centered innate drives are almost exclusively reserved for family members and close friends. Therefore, they can only be expressed in an atmosphere of reciprocal altruism. Again, true collaboration and the sharing of tacit knowledge takes place voluntarily and thus requires a shared-access context.

However uncomfortable such a "soft" approach may make leaders feel at first, it is the direction that will ultimately lead to organizational success and greater personal fulfillment because it is consistent with our evolutionary path. Humans have evolved into the most complex biological systems known to date. We have developed into the *ultimate* social creature by means of selective pressure, self-organization, and chance. In fact, we have a brain that has evolved specifically for maximum social interactions enhanced by our capacity to communicate verbally. Socialization is a survival mechanism for humans. Hence, we need to take full advantage of our strongest qualities instead of suppressing them in our organizations. Controlled-access context will not ultimately promote corporate learning, success, and longevity.

My ideas do not relate only to corporate entities; they can (and should) be applied to society in general. For example, we are raised in a stratified environment where self-centered drives persist. Altruism is not considered a favorable trait in a world dominated by consumerism. Obviously, these persistent self-centered traits are detrimental to our society as illustrated by the slaughter of innocent students and a faculty member at Columbine High School in Littleton, Colorado in the spring of 1999. Thus, only a committed societal change will allow us to reverse these trends. Once again, this change involves a conscious choice of a shared-access context where other-centered human drives are also nurtured and we forge an environment where attachment, affiliation, and care giving predominate over rank, territoriality, and possessions. Are we past the point of no return? I do not think so. Our society has created an alienating environment for our inherent genetic predispositions and, accordingly, we can also change it for the better.

The change, however, will not be easy. As previously mentioned, the circular causality created between the environment and expression of the innate drives is a self-reinforcing condition. Physical alterations of one's neuronal pathways will not be readily adapted in a short time frame. By changing to a shared-access, self-organizing environment, we cause our brains to go through experiential selection and reentrant mapping to express a balance between the self-centered and other-centered drives.

Because fundamental changes in biological systems can take years to develop, this process will not come about with a memo on Monday morning. Any efforts to adopt this system require a sustained commitment by *all* our social institutions. Continued education, communication, and commitment play a critical role in seeing the process through. Transitional leadership will also play an important role in this transformation; however, once achieved, the systems no longer should depend on position power but must rely on constantly changing situational leadership. Thus, for the new organizational framework to succeed, transitional leaders must work themselves out of a job. If they do not, ultimately no meaningful changes can take place, and organizational learning is again restrained.

This book is all about *unleashing our creative potential* or *unmanagement*. It advocates the development of a shared-access or self-organizing environment, fostering both sides of human nature for optimum intellectual capital generation. As in any true biological system, the outcomes cannot be anticipated, managed, or controlled. What we can affect is the environment that will promote the context required for the best sustainable advantages of the individual and the organization alike. To be successful in the third millennium, we must be capable of learning, adapting, and responding to our changing surroundings. Millions of years of evolution have allowed us to attain great flexibility as human beings; it is now time that we learn how to reapply bio-logic within our organizations.

Without the activation of the other-centered innate human drives, formal self-organization is not possible. Without voluntary collaboration, the inherent, tacit, creative potential within individual members of an organization cannot be actualized. The choice is ours whether we continue on the current self-centered path or learn to adopt more egalitarian modes of managing our resources, which are more in line with our evolutionary history and which are more effective for a knowledge society.

Human values such as love, truthfulness, fairness, freedom, unity, tolerance, responsibility, and respect for life are universal. These values need to be the fundamental tapestry of our organizations so that the altruistic side of human nature has an opportunity to be fully expressed along with our self-centered side. In the twentieth century, democracy has triumphed over other forms of government because it caters to our *humanness* in the most balanced fashion possible. Democratic principles provide the best means to close the gap between our unchanging human nature and the discontinuous environment we have created for ourselves. Will we have the foresight and courage to take advantage of its collaborative power to unleash human nature in pursuit of knowledge and general social well being in the corporate world and other social institutions in the future? We can affect our destiny, but we do not have to be the slaves of our own making.

Afterword

When Bill and I started W.L. Gore & Associates, Inc. on January 1, 1958, we dreamed of establishing a company based on products from a very special polytetrafluoroethylene (PTFE). More important to both of us was how we envisioned building an organization of associates dedicated to the success of this fledging enterprise. We wanted to know the people with whom we worked. Bill was convinced, from his previous work experience, that the potentials of people to contribute in significant ways to the organizational objectives were limited by the restrictive operative structures that were imposed by most large organizations of the day.

Now 41 years later, W.L. Gore & Associates, Inc. has become a highly successful multinational enterprise of nearly 6,000 associates. As I look back at the progress we have made, I clearly see that Bill was a visionary in his organizational thinking. With Bill's leadership, we were able to create an organization that was different in that we trusted people to do the "right thing" as opposed to putting complex control structures in place so that they couldn't do the "wrong thing." In my judgment, having four relatively simple operating principles was also crucial to our success. When I reflect back to the associates who joined our organization, I can't help but marvel at their extraordinary accomplishments. I know in my heart that our business philosophy contributed importantly to their ability and satisfaction of growing the enterprise.

Dr. Ehin has pointed out in his book that people are looking to participate in organizations where their inherent drives or motivations can be manifested to the mutual advantage of the organization and themselves. People want to be a part of an organization where they can grow in capability to contribute to the financial and organizational success and be recognized and rewarded for their contributions.

Genevieve W. Gore
Cofounder
W.L. Gore & Associates, Inc.

Glossary

Bio-logic The paradigm that living systems are designed to function in a self-organizing mode without externally imposed controls.

Circular causality The phenomenon where an organism affects its environment and in turn is influenced or altered by its surroundings—also known as *co-evolution*.

Controlled-access context Where access to the resources of a group is controlled by one or a few select individuals.

Core competencies The hard-to-coordinate diverse production or service skills and integrated multiple streams of people and technologies.

DNA molecule One of the 46 twisted, ladder-shaped (the famous double helix) molecules inside the nucleus of most human cells that contain the body's blueprints.

Explicit knowledge Knowledge that has been codified or formally defined. It is usually gained through formal education and training.

Genes Blueprints within the DNA molecule for making proteins.

Innate human drives Certain human predisposed and genetically determined behavior patterns in responding to specific environmental conditions. They are not instincts.

Instincts Automatic responses to the sudden changes in the immediate environment.

Machine-logic The paradigm that all systems, including living systems, function like machines or clockwork and, therefore, need to be externally controlled.

Other-centered innate drives Genetically affected behavior that is primarily concerned with the welfare of others.

Requisite variety The law of requisite variety stipulates that for a system to properly survive, it must be capable of matching whatever complexity its environment presents.

Self-centered innate drives Genetically affected behavior that is primarily concerned with self-preservation.

Self-organization Serendipitous and symbiotic relationships that develop among biological systems for mutual benefit and survival.

Shared-access context   Where resources of a group are equitably managed by all members of the group.

Tacit knowledge   Knowledge that is unrelated and not codified. It encompasses ideas and abstractions at the individual level. It is acquired by first-hand experiences and working with more experienced people.

Bibliography

Allman, J. and Brothers, L. (1994) "Faces, Fear and the Amygdala." *Nature*, December 15, pp. 613–614.

Angela, A. and Angela, P. (1993) *The Extraordinary Story of Human Origins*. Prometheus Books, Buffalo, NY.

Argyris, C. (1994) "Good Communication that Blocks Learning," *Harvard Business Review*, July–August, pp. 77–85.

Ashby, W.R. (1956) *An Introduction to Cybernetics*. Chapman and Hall, London, England.

Bailey, K. (1987) *Human Paleopsychology: Applications to Aggression and Pathological Processes*. Lawrence Erlbaum, Hove and London, Hillsdale, NJ.

Bakan, D. (1966) *The Duality of Human Existence*. Beacon Books, Boston, MA.

Barkow, J.H., Cosmides, L. and Toomby, J. (1995) *The Adapted Mind: Evolutionary Psychology and the Generation of Culture*. Oxford University Press, New York, NY.

Barlow, C., ed. (1994) *Evolution Extended: Biological Debates on the Meaning of Life*. MIT Press, Cambridge, MA.

Block, P. (1993) *Stewardship: Choosing Service Over Self-Interest*. Berrett-Koehler, San Francisco, CA.

Bouchard, T.J. (1994) "Genes, Environment and Personality," *Science*, Vol. 264, pp. 1700–1701.

Capra, F. (1982) *The Turning Point*. Simon & Schuster, New York, NY.

Case, J. (1997) "Opening the Books," *Harvard Business Review*, March–April, pp. 118–127.

Chance, M.R.A. (1988) "Introduction," in *Social Fabrics of the Mind*, edited by M.R.A. Chance. Lawrence Erlbaum, Hove and London, Hillsdale, NJ.

Collins, T.C. and Porras, T.I. (1994) *Built to Last: Successful Habits of Visionary Companies*. Harper Business, HarperCollins, New York, NY.

Colt, G.H. (1998) "Were You Born That Way?" *Life*, April, pp. 39–49.

Colvin, G. (1997) "The Changing Act of Becoming Unbeatable," *Fortune*, November 24, pp. 299–300.

Covey, S.R. (1989) *The 7 Habits of Highly Effective People.* Simon & Schuster, New York, NY.

Darwin, C. (1936) *The Origin of Species and the Descent of Man.* The Modern Library, New York, NY.

Davis, T.R.V. (1997) "Open-Book Management: Its Promise and Pitfalls," *Organizational Dynamics*, Winter, pp. 7–20.

Dorsey, D.E. (1997) "Escape from the Red Zone," *Fast Company*, April–May pp. 116–127.

Dunbar, R. (1996) *Grooming, Gossip, and the Evaluation of Language.* Harvard University Press, Cambridge, MA.

Durant, W. (1961) *The Story of Philosophy.* Simon & Schuster, New York, NY.

During, A.T. (1993) "Are We Happy Yet: How the Pursuit of Happiness Is Failing," *The Futurist*, January–February, pp. 20–24.

Edelman, G.M. (1992) *Bright Air, Brilliant Fire.* Basic Books, Harper Collins, New York, NY.

Ehin, C. (1998) "Fostering Both Sides of Human Nature—The Foundation for Collaborative Relationships," *Business Horizons*, May–June, pp. 15–25.

Ehin, C. (1995) "The Quest for Empowering Organizations: Some Lessons from Our Foraging Past," *Organization Science*, November–December, pp. 666–671.

Ehin, C. (1995) "The Ultimate Advantage of Self-Organizing Systems," *The Journal for Quality and Participation*, September, pp. 30–38.

Ehin, C. (1993) "A High-Performance Team Is Not a Multi-Part Machine," *The Journal for Quality and Participation*, December, pp. 38–48.

Eldredge, N. and Gould, S.J. (1972) "Punctuated Equilibria: An Alternative to Phyletic Gradualism." In *Models of Paleobiology*, edited by T.J.M. Schopf, pp. 82–115. Freeman, Cooper and Co., San Francisco, CA.

Emery, M., ed. (1993) *Participative Design for Participative Democracy.* Australia National University, Canberra, Australia.

Fagan, B.M. (1990) *The Journey from Eden.* Thames and Hudson, New York, NY.

Fletcher, J.K. (1996) "A Relational Approach to the Protean Worker." In *The Career Is Dead—Long Live the Career*, edited by Douglas T. Hall and Associates, pp. 115-124. Jossey-Bass, San Francisco, CA.

Fortey, R. (1997) *Life.* Knopf, New York, NY.

Fox, R. (1989) *The Search for Society: Quest for a Biosocial Science and Morality.* Rutgers University Press, New Brunswick, NJ.

Fulmer, R.M., Gibbs, P. and Keys, J.B. (1998) "The Second Generation Learning Organization: New Tools for Sustaining Competitive Advantage," *Organizational Dynamics*, Autumn, pp. 7–20.

Ghoshal, S. and Tsai, W. (1998) "Social Capital and Value Creation: The Role of Intrafirm Networks," *The Academy of Management Journal*, Vol. 41, No. 4, August, pp. 464–476.

Gore, R. (1997) "Tracking the First of Our Kind," *National Geographic*, Vol. 192, No. 3, pp. 92–99.

Gould, S.J. (1996) *Full House*. Harmony Books, New York, NY.

Gould, S.J. (1993) *Eight Little Piggies: Reflections in Natural History*. Norton, New York, NY.

Gross, B. (1998) "The New Math of Ownership," *Harvard Business Review*, November–December, pp. 68–74.

Haken, H. (1981) *The Science of Structure: Synergetics*. Van Nostrand Reinhold, New York, NY.

Halal, W.E., ed. (1998) *The Infinite Resource: Creating and Leading Knowledge Enterprises*. Jossey-Bass, San Francisco, CA.

Hallowell, E.M. (1999) "The Human Moment at Work," *Harvard Business Review*, January–February, pp. 58–66.

Hamson, N. et al. (1997) *After Atlantis: Working, Managing and Leading in Turbulent Times*. Butterworth–Heinemann, Boston, MA.

Hansen, T.M., Nohria, N. and Tierney, T. (1999) "What's Your Strategy for Managing Knowledge," *Harvard Business Review*, March–April, pp. 106–116.

Harris, M. (1989) "Life Without Chiefs," *New Age Journal*, November/December, pp. 42–45.

Heckman, F. (1997) "Designing Organizations for Flow Experiences," *Journal of Quality and Participation*, March, pp. 24–33.

Herbert, W. (1997) "Politics of Biology," *U.S. News & World Report*, April 21, pp. 72–80.

Herzberg, F. (1987) "One More Time: How Do You Motivate Employees?" *Harvard Business Review*, September–October, pp. 109–120.

Hitt, M.A., Keats, B.W. and DeMarie, S.M. (1998) "Navigating in the New Competitive Landscape: Building Strategic Flexibility and Competitive Advantage with 21st Century," *Academy of Management Executives*, November, pp. 22–43.

Hoecklin, L. (1995) *Managing Cultural Differences*. Addison-Wesley, New York, NY.

Homans, G. (1950) *The Human Group*. Harcourt Brace, New York, NY.

Johanson, D. and Johanson, L. (1994) *Ancestors: In Search of Human Origins*. Willard Books, New York, NY.

Joyce, R. (1992) "Global Hero," *International Management*, September, pp. 82–85.

Kauffman, S. (1995) *At Home in the Universe*. Oxford University Press, New York, NY.

Keidel, R.W. (1994) "Rethinking Organizational Design," *Academy of Management Executives*, Vol. 8, No. 4, pp.12–20.

Keller, E.F. and Lloyd, E.A., eds. (1992) *Keywords in Evolutionary Biology*. Harvard University Press, Cambridge, MA.

Kelly, K. (1998) *New Rules for The New Economy*. Viking, New York, NY.

Kelly, K. (1994) *Out of Control: The Rise of Neo-biological Civilization*. William Patrick Books, Addison-Wesley, New York, NY.

Kelso, J.A.S. (1995) *Dynamic Patterns: The Self-Organization of Brain and Behavior*. Bradford Books, MIT Press, Cambridge, MA.

Kiernan, M.J. (1993) "The New Strategic Architecture: Learning to Compete in the Twenty-first Century," *Academy of Management Executives*, Vol. 7, No. 1, pp. 7–21.

Kim, C. and Mauborgne, R. (1997) "Fair Process: Managing in the Knowledge Economy," *Harvard Business Review*, July–August, pp. 65–75.

Kitcher, P. (1996) *The Lives to Come: The Genetic Revolution and Human Possibilities*. Simon & Schuster, New York, NY.

Klein, E.H. and Izzo, J.B. (1998) *Awakening Corporate Soul*. Fairwinds Press, New York, NY.

Kofman, F. and Senge, P.M. (1993) "Communities of Learning: The Heart of Learning Organizations," *Organizational Dynamics*, Fall, pp. 5–23.

Kohn, A. (1998) "How Incentives Undermine Performance," *The Journal for Quality and Participation*, March–April, pp. 7–13.

Kohn, A. (1992) *No Contest: The Case Against Competition*. Houghton Mifflin, New York, NY.

Leakey, R. and Lewin, R. (1995) *The Sixth Extinction: Patterns of Life and the Future of Humankind*. Doubleday, New York, NY.

Leakey, R. and Lewin, R. (1992) Origins Reconsidered: In Search of What Makes Us Human. Doubleday, New York, NY.

Lee, R.B. (1979) *The !Kung San: Men, Women and Work in a Foraging Society*. Cambridge University Press, London, England.

Leonard-Barton, D. (1995) *Wellsprings of Knowledge: Building and Sustaining the Sources of Innovation*. Harvard Business School Press, Boston, MA.

MacLean, P.D. (1973) *A Triune Concept of the Brain Behavior*. University of Toronto Press, Toronto, Canada.

Mann, C.C. (1994) "Behavioral Genetics in Transition," *Science*, Vol. 264, pp. 1686–1689.

Marshall, L. (1976) *The !Kung of Nyae Nyae*. Harvard University Press, Cambridge, MA.

Mascarenhas, B., Baveja, A. and Jamil, M. (1998) "Dynamic Core Competencies in Leading Multinational Companies," *California Management Review*, Vol. 40. No. 4, Summer, pp 117–132.

Monastersky, R. (1998) "The Rise of Life on Earth," *National Geographic*, March, pp. 54–81.

Nahapiet, J. and Ghoshal, S. (1998) "Social Capital, Intellectual Capital, and the Organizational Advantage," *The Academy of Management Review*, March, pp. 242–266.

Nesse, R.M. and Lloyd, A.T. (1992) "The Evolution of Psychodynamic Mechanisms." In *Keywords in Evolutionary Biology*, pp. 601–626. Harvard University Press, Cambridge, MA.

Nicholson, N. (1997) "Evolutionary Psychology: Toward a New View of Human Nature and Organizational Society," *Human Relations*, Vol. 50, No. 9, pp.1053–1078.

Ornstein, R. (1986) *Multimind*. Houghton Mifflin, Boston, MA.

Ouchi, W. (1981) *Theory Z*. Avon Books, New York, NY.

Petzinger, T., Jr. (1999) *The New Pioneers*. Simon & Schuster, New York, NY.

Petzinger, T., Jr. (1997) "Self-Organization Will Free Employees to Act Like Bosses," *Wall Street Journal*, January 3, p. 31.

Pfeffer, T. and Veiga, T.F. (1999) "Putting People First for Organizational Success," *Academy of Management Executives*, Vol. 13, No. 2, May, pp. 37–48.

Pollack, R. (1994) *Signs of Life: The Language and Meaning of DNA*. Houghton Mifflin, New York, NY.

Power, M. (1991) *The Egalitarians—Human and Chimpanzee*. Cambridge University Press, New York, NY.

Prahalad, C.K. and Hamel, G. (1990) "The Core Competence of the Corporation," *Harvard Business Review*, May–June, pp. 79–91.

Raup, D.M. (1991) *Extinction: Bad Genes or Bad Luck?* Norton, New York, NY.

Restak, R. (1984) *The Brain*. Bantam Books, New York, NY.

Robbins, H. and Finnley, M. (1995) *Why Teams Don't Work*. Peterson's/Pacesetter Books, Princeton, NJ.

Sagan, C. (1977) *The Dragons of Eden*. Random House, New York, NY.

Schrof, J. (1997) "What Is a Memory Made Of?" *U.S. News & World Report*, August 25, pp. 71–73.

Senge, P. (1998) "Teaching an Organization to Learn," *News for a Change* (published by the Association for Quality and Participation), March, pp. 1, 9.

Senge, P. (1990) "The Leader's New Work: Building Learning Organizations," *Sloan Management Review*, Fall, pp. 7–23.

Spreitzer, G. (1996) "Social Structural Characteristics of Psychologic Empowerment," *Academy of Management Journal*, April, Vol. 39(2), pp. 485–504.

Stevens, A. and Price, T. (1996) *Evolutionary Psychiatry: A New Beginning*. Routledge, New York, NY.

Stewart, T.A. (1997) *Intellectual Capital: The New Wealth of Organizations*. Doubleday/Currency, New York, NY.

Sveiby, K.E. (1997) *The New Organizational Wealth: Managing & Measuring Knowledge-Based Assets*. Berrett-Koehler, San Francisco, CA.

Toffler, A. (1982) *The Third Wave*. Bantam Books, New York, NY.

Toomby, J. and Cosmides, L. (1992) "The Psychological Foundations of Culture." In *Keywords in Evolutionary Biology*, pp. 3-117. Harvard University Press, Cambridge, MA.

Wageman, R. (1997) "Critical Success Factors for Creating Superb Self-Managing Teams," *Organizational Dynamics*, Summer, pp. 49–61.

Wheatley, M.J. (1992) *Leadership and the New Science: Learning About Organization from an Orderly Universe*. Berrett-Koehler, San Francisco, CA.

Wheatley, M. and Keller-Rogers, M. (1995) "Breathing Life Into Organizations," *The Journal for Quality and Participation*, July–August, pp. 6–10.

Williams, G. (1966) *Adaption and Natural Selection*. Princeton University Press, Princeton, NJ.

Wilson, E.O. (1998) *Consilience: The Unity of Knowledge*. Knopf, New York, NY.

Wright, R. (1996) "Science and Original Sin," *Time*, October 28, pp. 76–77.

Yellen, J.E. (1990) "The Transformation of the Kalahari Kung," *Scientific American*, April, pp. 99–105.

Index

Butterworth-Heinemann Business Books for Transforming Business

5th Generation Management: Co-creating Through Virtual Enterprising, Dynamic Teaming, and Knowledge Networking, Revised Edition,
Charles M. Savage, 0-7506-9701-6

After Atlantis: Working, Managing, and Leading in Turbulent Times,
Ned Hamson, 0-7506-9884-5

The Alchemy of Fear: How to Break the Corporate Trance and Create Your Company's Successful Future,
Kay Gilley, 0-7506-9909-4

Beyond Business as Usual: Practical Lessons in Accessing New Dimensions,
Michael W. Munn, 0-7506-9926-4

Beyond Strategic Vision: Effective Corporate Action with Hoshin Planning,
Michael Cowley and Ellen Domb, 0-7506-9843-8

Beyond Time Management: Business with Purpose,
Robert A. Wright, 0-7506-9799-7

The Breakdown of Hierarchy: Communicating in the Evolving Workplace,
Eugene Marlow and Patricia O'Connor Wilson, 0-7506-9746-6

Business and the Feminine Principle: The Untapped Resource,
Carol R. Frenier, 0-7506-9829-2

Choosing the Future: The Power of Strategic Thinking,
Stuart Wells, 0-7506-9876-4

Conscious Capitalism: Principles for Prosperity,
David A. Schwerin, 0-7506-7021-5

Corporate DNA: Learning from Life,
Ken Baskin, 0-7506-9844-6

Cultivating Common Ground: Releasing the Power of Relationships at Work,
Daniel S. Hanson, 0-7506-9832-2

Flight of the Phoenix: Soaring to Success in the 21st Century,
John Whiteside and Sandra Egli, 0-7506-9798-9

Getting a Grip on Tomorrow: Your Guide to Survival and Success in the Changed World of Work,
    Mike Johnson, 0-7506-9758-X

Innovation Strategy for the Knowledge Economy: The Ken Awakening,
    Debra M. Amidon, 0-7506-9841-1

Innovation Through Intuition: The Hidden Intelligence,
    Sandra Weintraub, 0-7506-9937-X

The Intelligence Advantage: Organizing for Complexity,
    Michael D. McMaster, 0-7506-9792-X

Intuitive Imagery: A Resource at Work,
    John B. Pehrson and Susan E. Mehrtens, 0-7506-9805-5

The Knowledge Evolution: Expanding Organizational Intelligence,
    Verna Allee, 0-7506-9842-X

Leadership in a Challenging World: A Sacred Journey,
    Barbara Shipka, 0-7506-9750-4

Leading Consciously: A Pilgrimage Toward Self Mastery,
    Debashis Chatterjee, 0-7506-9864-0

Leading from the Heart: Choosing Courage over Fear in the Workplace,
    Kay Gilley, 0-7506-9835-7

Learning to Read the Signs: Reclaiming Pragmatism in Business,
    F. Byron Nahser, 0-7506-9901-9

Leveraging People and Profit: The Hard Work of Soft Management,
    Bernard A. Nagle and Perry Pascarella, 0-7506-9961-2

Marketing Plans That Work: Targeting Growth and Profitability,
    Malcolm H.B. McDonald and Warren J. Keegan, 0-7506-9828-4

A Place to Shine: Emerging from the Shadows at Work,
    Daniel S. Hanson, 0-7506-9738-5

Power Partnering: A Strategy for Business Excellence in the 21st Century,
    Sean Gadman, 0-7506-9809-8

Putting Emotional Intelligence to Work: Successful Leadership Is More Than IQ,
    David Ryback, 0-7506-9956-6

Resources for the Knowledge-Based Economy Series
    The Knowledge Economy,
        Dale Neef, 0-7506-9936-1
    Knowledge Management and Organizational Design,
        Paul S. Myers, 0-7506-9749-0
    Knowledge Management Tools,
        Rudy L. Ruggles, III, 0-7506-9849-7
    Knowledge in Organizations,
        Laurence Prusak, 0-7506-9718-0
    The Strategic Management of Intellectual Capital,
        David A. Klein, 0-7506-9850-0

The Rhythm of Business: The Key to Building and Running Successful Companies,
    Jeffrey C. Shuman, 0-7506-9991-4

Setting the PACE® in Product Development: A Guide to Product and Cycle-time Excellence,
    Michael E. McGrath, 0-7506-9789-X

Time to Take Control: The Impact of Change on Corporate Computer Systems,
    Tony Johnson, 0-7506-9863-2

The Transformation of Management,
    Mike Davidson, 0-7506-9814-4

What Is the Emperor Wearing? Truth-Telling in Business Relationships,
    Laurie Weiss, 0-7506-9872-1

Who We Could Be at Work, Revised Edition,
    Margaret A. Lulic, 0-7506-9739-3

Working from Your Core: Personal and Corporate Wisdom in a World of Change,
    Sharon Seivert, 0-7506-9931-0

Business Climate Shifts: Profiles of Change Makers,
    Warner Burke and William Trahant, 0-7506-7186-6

Large Scale Organizational Change: An Executive's Guide,
    Christopher Laszlo and Jean-Francois Laugel, 0-7506-7230-7

To purchase any Butterworth-Heinemann title,
please visit your local bookstore or call 1-800-366-2665.